MERCH

RE

BY BOB JACKMAN

Also available from,
Bob Jackman
1 Barmoor Lane
Scarborough
North Yorkshire
YO13 0NX

CONTENTS

A DEDICATION

I know many of my old shipmates must by now have retired from the sea. As I write this, I am eighty-three years old and like them I battered my weary way round the world many times from 1950 to 1990. I retired but couldn't sit watching the telly every day, so, when the opportunity presented itself I became the village newsagent. I found time to do oil paintings that made money, and also joined a drama club to write, act and direct plays. Now I just write books. I also found playing darts was a lot easier and much more profitable in the nice, steady local pub than it was in the smoke room of a rolling ship.

I have never known an ancient mariner yet, deck, engine or catering who couldn't tell a great story when he had finished his second beer. But why don't they write them down? From there, why don't they publish them?

In Kingussie, when the last tourist has gone home, the villagers become united in joining clubs for knitting scarves, socks, jumpers, and other woollen goodies. Local pubs have darts teams and form leagues, they have races on skis, writing classes and drama groups to entertain themselves until the tourists return in the spring.

The Village Drama Group in Kingussie expanded from being a Writers Group and we put on plays in our village hall, plays that were well attended.

In Kingussie, there is an old folk's home run by nuns and, at the Mother Superior's request, two of us once put on a funny play that had everyone laughing until the tears ran down their faces.

While the oldies were being finally bedded down for the night, the Mother Superior took us into her office and poured out two very large whiskies. She might have known how to run an old folks home but she had no idea where to stop as she poured out our whiskies.

When given a part in a new play, we learned our lines completely and were shamed if we didn't get them perfect by the following week. After proving to be word perfect, movements and actions were taught at the next meeting. We learned that a mere turn of a hand could be as important as a spoken word and a facial expression could change a scene.

We had one twenty-five-year old twit employed in the Village Council Offices, who didn't appear at rehearsals then informed us on the night before the show he had changed his mind and didn't want to appear in the play.

This caused a panic, but after a few dozen telephone calls, we found a Chief Police Inspector in Dumfries who promised to take the part and, bless his soul, he arrived in our village next day at lunchtime, read the part through a few times and played it beautifully that night.

The Drama Group also played in surrounding villages.

In later years my parents moved from their home town of Glasgow to Scarborough and because of their advanced years, my dear wife Mary and I left the Highlands of Bonnie Scotland and moved down to be with them.

A Booker Prize winner who we found was not a Booker Prize winner opened up a class in the nearby town of Pickering and after his second lesson it was obvious he knew as much about writing stories as a haddock knows about repairing bicycles. It was the class's unanimous request that he left.

The others knew I had some past experience in writing stories so they asked me to take the class and consequently I became teacher.

One girl in the class called 'Mary' told us how a hedge separated her long back garden from the beer garden next door. She was on her knees, weeding, when a child's voice whispered 'Hello', from the other side of the hedge.

'Oh, hello,' Mary replied. 'What is your name?'

'My name is Jennifer and I am four.'

The conversation continued with Mary on her knees weeding until she finally stood up and leaned over the hedge to see her companion.

The four year old Jennifer looked up at her, deeply disappointed. 'I thought you were a rabbit!' she cried.

I pushed Mary into offering her story to a magazine. She sent it to Readers Digest, they published it and she received a cheque for **£150.** That was her start in a very lucrative pastime, the pastime of writing more stories.

On two occasions, I took one of Yorkshire's most talented authors, the celebrated Frances Anne Bond, with me to my group in Pickering to give a lesson. She spoke on many subjects, including how to be a successful trout fisher and she didn't know one end of a trout rod from the other. She had a lovely personality and that shone through in her writing.

Another pupil was a farmer's wife, a slender, beautiful creature who arrived late at the class. 'The gale force winds last night blew the roof off our barn. I was up all night helping to cover it with big canvas tarpaulins. I got blown off the roof twice!'

'Write it!'

'Write it?'

'Write it!'

'Farmer's Weekly' published it, sent her four copies of the magazine and a cheque for **£40**. I learned she is writing in farmers magazines quite regularly now and her earnings are now quite a bit higher than a mere **£40.**

Jenny worked at Flamingo Land. She didn't talk much, didn't think much of people but she had a gift of communicating with animals. Animals loved her and all animals obeyed her. Wild deer that fled at the sight of humans would quietly stand and let her stroke them.

She went one day to sheep-dog trials as a spectator, taking a young collie with her. Her young collie became over-excited, exploded into a flock of sheep and scattered them all over the hill side.

She told us the story, I told her to sell it and she made £35.

The point I am making here is that each one of those story tellers told me, quote, 'Oh, I could never write a story. Oh, Bob, I could never write a story.'

Those of us who served in the Merchant Navy have terrific experiences to look back on over the years; ports in far corners of the world, life on board old ships or new ships, tales of 'affairs' with ladies of different nationalities and all kinds of adventures, so instead of being a retired nonentity stuck in front of the telly all day, why not join a writers group? Why not start to write a book?

Art classes? You meet people, you paint pictures, you sell your work and you are not bored to tears with a retired life. Ever heard of Picasso?

I left the sea in 1990 and boredom has never had a chance to be a problem with me. Don't let your retirement from the sea be a problem to you.

Write a book. A retired seaman has a thousand things to write about.

I remember a story old Chief Engineer Alexandre told me. He said it was a summer's day and he was tidying the front garden when a very attractive lady appeared at his garden gate.

'Mister Alexandre?'

He smiled and looked at her over the top of his glasses. 'Aye.'

'Simon Alexandre? Formerly Chief Engineer in Shell Tankers?'

'Aye, that's right.'

'How lovely! You sailed with my mother's husband in some ships. You remember Tommy Walker? You were good friends.'

'Aye, I remember Tommy. I met up with him on many ships. We all met up on leave sometimes too. So he's your father?'

'No, he's not my father. He is my mother's husband.' She smiled at him and moved closer. 'My mother says you are my father.'

Have you heard stories like that? Or have you heard stories that are not like that?

Write them down, publish them and the profits will help to boost your Merchant Navy Officers Pension Fund.

THIS TAX BUSINESS

It began in the mid-1950s when I was caught in a crash where three cars were involved. It took place on a sharp bend at the top of a short steep hill near Glasgow and involved two pals and myself. My lovely old Wolseley 6/80 was a wreck and there was some confusion about insurance. I had not caused the crash, the guilty party's insurance was worthless and I was not recompensed for the loss of my car by the guilty party or by my own car insurance company.

The months went by waiting for the case to go to court, the haggling between insurance companies was time consuming and the time wasted was a drain on my finances. The insurance companies were still grimly but politely haggling with each other while the figures in my bank book were decreasing.

I was twenty-five years old, a student with MacGibbon's College of Marine Engineering in those far-off days, studying for my Board of Trade Qualifications in Marine Engineering Second Class. But a car was a necessity and being engineers in the mid-1950s we could pick up a bargain of sorts at Glasgow Motor Car Auctions. I was escorted and supported by two knowledgeable seafaring students, Louis Dupre and Bertie Wilson.

One could gain further engineering experience in overhauling, maintaining and driving a motor car that cost a lot less than £100 and my two pals and I would benefit with the engineering experience.

She was a little 1935 Morris Eight, the auctioneer asked for five pounds, I put up my hand, my pal Bert nudged me and whispered 'go to six,' the auctioneer said six, I said 'seven' the auctioneer said 'seven' and the car was mine.

Bert wasn't bidding. He was assisting me but his assistance raised my antiquated little Morris car price by 30%.

Bert and Louis were two of my staunchest pals. Bert hailed from the town of Macduff in the far north of Scotland and Louis was from Mauritius somewhere in the Indian Ocean, two handsome louts who liked their beer, they liked the ladies but their studies had priority over their pleasures.

In those distant days, the income tax of Merchant Navy Officers was handled by a tax office in Cardiff and I, encumbered with thermo-dynamical and mathematical studies relating to all matters of propulsion and maintenance of ship mechanisation, coupled with the horror of my car accident and the deceitful car insurance companies involved, probably made a complete cock of filling in my tax forms.

It was eight o'clock on a bright summer morning when I called to collect Louis at his basement flat in one of the roughest, but cheapest, districts of Glasgow. No locks on doors, no keys required, Louis lying fully dressed on his bunk surrounded by note books, John Lamb's 'Running and Maintenance of the Marine Diesel Engine,' Sothern's 'Verbal Notes and Sketches,' MacGibbon's Orals, C.C. Pounder's something or other and a host of similar works on marine engineering theory and practice. Masses of hand written sheets of paper lay scattered on the bed cover and linoleum for those were the days before computers.

Students studied as long as their eyes could stay open and daylight or night time hours were of very little consequence. Why didn't we go for politics or accountancy where a good night's sleep and high salaries were normal?

I wakened him with a bacon butty and a pint carton of milk.

'Up time! Let's go.'

He groaned, rubbed his bleary eyes, pulled on his shoes and, burdened with John Lamb's 'Running and Maintenance of the Marine Diesel Engine,' joined me in my little Morris Eight. I headed south and he went back to sleep.

We were well over the border when he wakened. 'Where are we going?'

'Cardiff.'

He digested this for a few minutes and went back to sleep again. Another hour passed, he yawned mightily, stretched and asked, 'What for?'

'Income tax.'

Then it was his turn to do the driving and my little Morris screamed down the A1 at nearly thirty-two miles an hour. As we arrived in Cardiff, the clutch had had enough, so we limped into a garage/filling station and a most obliging mechanic drove us to the Income Tax Office in his own car.

I achieved nothing. Two surly tax officials behind a wire screen talked a lot of bureaucratic gobble-de-gook, both speaking at the same time, pointing at paragraphs of small print in wads of forms, producing more forms, we couldn't get a word in, so we surrendered and made our way back to the garage.

The mechanic had just finished working on the clutch. 'Well, how did you get on with the blighters in the Merchant Navy Income Tax Office? You are Merchant Navy? Yeah, I thought so. My son's Merchant Navy. I've fixed your clutch. It will last until you get to Glasgow. No charge.'

'No charge?'

‘No charge. The blighters in the Merchant Navy Income Tax Offices just give Cardiff a bad name.’

So we set off back to Bonnie Scotland where Louis unintentionally bumped into a sheep that had trotted out in front of us. He said ‘sorry’ but I am not sure if it was to me, the car or the sheep. Otherwise it was a quiet run.

The subject of income tax came up in the college and we learned that the office in Cardiff did all Merchant Navy Taxation. My problem was two letters from two clerks from the same office in the same week, where the two clerks sent me highly informative statements contradicting each other. We believe they were often reprimanded for incompetence by other income tax offices in the country. Great!

However the little Morris Eight did serve me well, I passed all the exams, received my ‘Second’s Ticket’ and left to join the MV ‘City of Poona’ as Second Engineer Officer. When I joined, all the money I possessed in the world was in my right hand trouser pocket and it included the tenner I was given for my dear Morris.

In August 1958 I joined the MV Inchmull of Williamson’s of Hong Kong and earned a much higher wage than I did in City Line.

It was a much higher wage, but I earned every penny of it. We sailed on the China coast, Shanghai to Chingwantao and back on the coal run, where Chinese commando dockers wrecked the winches as fast as we could repair them. In the winter season, the old Inchmull ploughed her way through sheet ice and those that were not on watch in the engine room were out in the ice and snow repairing winches.

The temperature in winter on the China coast could fall to minus 40 degrees Centigrade or Fahrenheit. (They are both the same.)

In 1956 we were hit by the big typhoon 'Wanda', the one that reached two hundred and something miles an hour. It caught us between Formosa and the mainland then blasted up Napier Road in Hong Kong making Napier Road look like the River Ganges in a monsoon.

But the money was good. The money was very good.

When it came time to go home, one could take a stroll down Ice House Street in Hong Kong to the tax office. Being outside the United Kingdom for a full financial year meant you had that year tax free and Hong Kong income tax could be paid with some of the loose change in one's trouser pocket. We learned that later.

I sailed on the 'Inchmull', 'Inchstuart', 'Inchstaffa', 'Ardmore', and 'Ardtara' paying Hong Kong Income Tax, a total of fifteen years under conditions that would make the most sadistic of tax men weep at their loss.

I began my time with Scottish Ship Management, but my past was catching up with me and my health broke down.

I loved engines, I loved the Merchant Navy and I sailed with some of the finest gentlemen that ever wielded a spanner or used a sextant but it all had been too much. My blood pressure had rocketed and I had a long spell in the Merchant Navy Dreadnought Hospital in London getting it down to normal.

But there is something called the 'Memory Bank.'

I can clearly remember events and work mates in my five year apprenticeship in Barclay Curle's Engine Works on the Clyde from 1945 to 1950. I remember details about my first ship, the MV 'Marjata', and all the other ships and fellows I sailed with over my forty-one years at sea. Those forty-one seafaring years ended in June 1990.

I remember my pal Louis, my co-driver on the Cardiff run in 1956. I met him in 1979 in Glasgow when I was 'standing by' a ship and he had nonchalantly strolled on board.

He had failed all his Board of Trade exams, had no qualifications, didn't like getting his hands dirty and was now a paint salesman.

'Not just ordinary paint, Bob, a marine paint, specially manufactured for ship's hulls, made in Hamburg, far superior to anything made in the UK. My basis wage is about equal to yours but when I make a sale as I often do, it doubles. And if I make two sales? Wow!! It takes a lot of paint to paint a ship's hull.'

I learned he works his own hours, travels all over the Continent, is given a new car of his choice every two years and the German head office handles his expenses and his income tax.

It was great to see one of my old pals from the distant past. We shook hands very firmly and he left, driving off in his new Mercedes. I wonder if he ever had a kind thought for my Morris Eight all those years ago. I wonder if I could get a job selling paint.

This 'memory bank' caused by my rocketed high blood pressure inspired me into writing about my days in the Merchant Navy. In 2003 I started to write about them, days that I could recall with crystal clarity.

Once I reached my early seventies, the memory that served me so well over the years went limp. I find I cannot recall the name of my next door neighbour, where I left the car in a car park, what my Barclay Card pin number is etc.

But I can remember everything I did thirty or forty years ago. Consequently my encounter with a shark in Indonesia prompted me to write about it and I put my other far off memories into print also.

My book 'SHARK' was published in 2004 by a publisher's widow living on her pension and little else so I waived all profits. Now, in 2013, 'SHARK' is still helping her pension immensely.

This prompted me to write 'Merchant Navy: Heroes and Half Wits', 'Merchant Navy, What a Life!' and I am now on this book, Book Four, as yet untitled. I can remember so much of the past, I can remember it all so clearly, but now, I am not even sure what day it is or what I had for dinner yesterday.

I might survive to my eighty-fourth birthday, but if I don't, I've certainly lived damned well for eighty-three of them!

DAYS ON THE DOLE

I am now a tired eighty-three year old and my computer and I live together in a modern two-bedroom flat in Scarborough. I have no relatives within two hundred miles in any direction and I am the last of our line with the name 'Jackman.'

To begin, I was born in a tiny two roomed flat on the top floor of a tenement in Glasgow in 1929 where we shared a toilet with two other families. Glasgow was a city of tenement buildings designed in this fashion.

The whole of Great Britain was in the crushing grip of mass unemployment and my father walked three miles in all weathers to collect our Family Unemployment Benefit, commonly referred to as 'Dole Money.' He then walked the three miles back to hand my mother the envelope, unopened. She would open it and line up the coins on the high mantelpiece, muttering, quote, 'rent, groceries, savings, gas.' The sixpence left over went to my Dad for his week's tobacco.

In think I must have been about four years old when one day I heard him say to my Mother; 'I don't need the sixpence, Mary. Christmas is coming up; you'll need money for the children's Christmas presents.' The children referred to were my sister and me and she was six years older.

I know I must have been about four years of age when he said those words, but I do remember them so clearly and I always will.

Where other men spent long hours standing at the street corner doing nothing or playing 'pitch and toss' for pennies, my dad was above that. He was also above drinking in the local public bars where many men spent all their dole money and staggered homewards, blind drunk with nothing left to feed their families on.

I remember one Saturday evening I was walking home with my Dad when a furious, helpless drunk outside the Corporation Woodside Timber Yard was being teased by a small group of children. Had that drunken fool managed to get a grip on any one of the children the result could have been serious.

'Wait here, Bobby.' My Dad spoke softly.

He walked over to the drunk, gripped him by the seat of his trousers and the back of his jacket collar and frog marched him into the timber yard and along to the stables. Minutes later he returned and closed the main gate behind him.

At home he told my Mother that he had dumped a drunk into a stable with one of the horses.

'Will he be safe enough there, Willie?'

'Aye, Mary. He'll be there until the workers arrive and let him out on Monday morning. I bolted the stable door behind him.'

Being unemployed meant he had little to do all day, so he passed the time doing scientific experiments at the kitchen sink where, to my astonishment, he could make water flow up a plastic tube into a bottle. Or he would have two bottles connected with a plastic tube and make water flow up and over from one bottle to the other.

This fascinated me tremendously.

Buying toys on our limited finances was out of the question so he made aeroplanes out of cardboard, painted them to make the cardboard as hard as plastic and, with a cardboard propeller and an elastic band, he could make them fly in circles, suspended from the washing pulley that ran across our ceiling. I also remember the jet engine he made, using a flat tin with a screw top lid as the boiler, a piece of copper pipe and a piece of candle to perform as the boiler furnace. This jet engine was mounted on a piece of wood shaped as a boat and it did move it from one end of our kitchen sink to the other, a distance of eighteen inches less boat length.

The tenements had a back yard that was used by the nine families in the flats to hang out their washing. It sloped downhill and thereby permanently provided us with a stagnant puddle for most of the year, nearly five foot long and three foot wide. All my pals came to see my steamship sailing majestically from one end of the puddle to the other. Sometimes their fathers came too.

During its construction and wash basin trials, there were a few problems to overcome, the main ones being my mother wanting to peel potatoes for our dinner or wash the dishes when we had finished.

I was fascinated by it all and it was probably due to my Dad's amazing scientific experiments with little pieces of piping, tin, painted cardboard and making water flow upwards in defiance of gravity that steered my adolescent brain towards being an engineer.

As a Second Engineer in later years, I felt the same exhilaration when I succeeded in curing any problems in a six-cylinder, 8,000 BHP Doxford marine engine as I did watching my Dad's jet engine driven boat successfully move the whole length of our back yard puddle.

In my days as a fourteen-year old in secondary school I was always in the top three in Mathematics, Science and Technical Subjects. We had fifty-one in our class and I think my Dad's scientific experiments at the kitchen sink were what inspired me in those three subjects.

(I also achieved a distinction in the school's Third Year Examinations by achieving a mere 9% in history. That was the lowest mark any pupil ever achieved in any subject since the days when the school was first built back in the dark ages.)

I had few toys. In fact, my only toy I remember as a child was a 'Trix Meccano Set', an assortment of metal girders, beams, wheels, angle bars etc., with a pack of nuts and bolts. When a birthday came up, I was presented with extra Trix sets and I never tired of building marvellous things. When it was time for bed, my Dad took over and he built marvellous things too.

All this was part of my early childhood and probably another brick in the foundation of me turning to engineering as I grew older. I played card games with my pals, went to the movies with my pals and joined in all kinds of pastimes with my pals but my interests in engineering, science and technology were the most important.

In 1911, my father was eleven years old when his father disappeared and many years later it was discovered he had departed from the United Kingdom and immigrated to America. My Dad was forced to become the eleven-year-old breadwinner of the family by delivering bread rolls round the houses from the local baker before going to school. Being late for school meant he was punished with the school teacher's long leather strap.

After school, he raced home for something to eat before going to his next job as sweeper-up, message boy and odd-job man in the local barber shop until it closed at 11.00 pm.

Quite often his Mother used his hard earned money to buy herself some new clothes when she felt like it, leaving little to feed her four children.

I lived with the poverty and hardship my parents went through in the days of mass unemployment, but I also absorbed all the knowledge I learned from my Dad's scientific experiments at the kitchen sink.

In 1945 I started my apprenticeship in engineering in Barclay Curle's Marine Engine Works on the Clydeside, earning twenty-four shillings a week. My pals earned seven pounds a week shovelling coal in the Springburn Railway Yards. If it started to rain, they sat in a goods wagon and played cards. If the rain stopped, they often just continued playing cards for a few hours longer.

With their high wages, their evenings were spent with girls, dances, movies and betting shops. My evenings were spent in evening classes or at home with books on marine diesel engines and auxiliaries and boilers and electro-technology and naval architecture and thermo-dynamics and a few other subjects I have long forgotten.

I remember the men I worked with in Barclay Curle's Engine Works, great men that made Clyde built ships and engines world famous, yet they carried sandwiches for their lunch and drank tea from a tea-can that had been boiled over a rivet fire. Was this to be my future?

Working conditions for apprentices were difficult. I was one who travelled by tramcar from Possilpark in the north of Glasgow to the engine works in Whiteinch in the west of Glasgow. I was late twice during my five years apprenticeship.

Three nights a week I went to Glasgow High School Evening Classes, which meant I rushed from the engine works in Whiteinch to my home in Possilpark, had a wash to get some of the dirt off me, a bite to eat and a dash to the High School Evening Classes in the centre of Glasgow. My weary body was delighted when it was bed time.

I suppose, subconsciously, that I still had visions of the poverty of the Depression in my mind and I wanted to be sure that should there be another national disaster like the one in the 1930s I would have qualifications that would get me a job and put food on my table.

My Dad, with his experiments at the kitchen sink was the basis of my learning without realising it. He, though uneducated through lack of schooling, gave me a future when other fathers left their sons to do as they pleased.

But I often think of how many of today's young people who know nothing about life in the Merchant Navy could be taught by those who are now retired.

Or have we left it too late?

TOOTHACHE

In the dining saloon the roast beef was good, the Yorkshire puddings were great and we were all in good spirits. There was ice cream with apple pie to follow when EEEEEEEE!!! **##++ I got toothache!

My whole jaw was in agony and my mouth was still full of roast beef and its accompaniments. I mumbled some excuses that no one understood and made my way to my cabin. I knew the next port was two weeks away and the next port may not even have a dentist. In a situation like that there are so many shipmates from the engine, deck and catering departments who are more than willing to assist in the business of removing a tooth from a fellow officer.

In my first thirty-two years in ships I had one occasion where I had to pull out an offending molar. I was Fourth Engineer. Big Charlie Quinn, our Fifth Engineer, was the first who was so extremely eager to offer his services with a pair of engine room pliers but I declined and he sulked.

This time I borrowed Third Engineer / Electrician Gordon Thomson's pliers to perform the excruciating task since his pliers would certainly be much cleaner than any I might find in the engine room workshop. Since I didn't want to make a show of how I might react extracting a back tooth I went down the engine room to the top store room and tried to gather some courage.

Eventually I gripped the offending molar in the jaws of the pliers and tried twisting it a little.

It was then I noticed the little Indian boiler man standing in the boiler flat watching me. He was balancing on tip toe with his left foot, his right foot wrapped round his left leg, the fist on his right arm was rammed deep inside his mouth and his left fist was clenched on top of his head. He looked quite pale for a Bengali.

Thirty minutes later the tooth was out.

I was returning the Third's pliers when Bill Underwood, Second Engineer, appeared with a large glass of whisky. 'Bob! Here's a spot of medication from our Chief, no less.'

I was holding the glass and showing Bill the hole in my gum when the Chief appeared in the cabin door. 'Did ye gi'e him the whisky yet?'

I hadn't had the whisky yet but Frank Findlay, Bill Underwood, Gordon Thomson and Tom Jones were still surveying the inside of my mouth where the faulty tooth had been. I still hadn't had a drop of the whisky.

When the Chief took out his pipe and lit it, the distraction allowed me to knock back the whisky, swill it around my mouth and let it burn my gum where the tooth had been.

The Chief puffed on his pipe for a moment. 'I remember on one ship many years ago, the Second Mate got a bad bout of toothache. He was a clever young bloke. I'll tell you what he did. He took a couple of ice cubes from the freezer and used them to freeze the inside of his mouth where the tooth was. Then the twit of the Mate took over.'

I looked at the others. 'He froze his jaw. Hell, why didn't I think of that?'

The Chief shook his head. 'It didn't do much good. We all held the Second Mate down and the Mate took the pliers and pulled out the wrong tooth.'

Some years passed and I applied similar tactics to remove one of my back teeth. I took a large whisky, an ice cube, took a large whisky, locked my cabin door, took a large whisky, pulled out the offending tooth and had a large whisky.

Another toothy tale? I remember some of us meeting a retired dentist in a dock side pub Port Adelaide and this was his story.

'A big BP oil tanker anchored outside the three mile limit here. It was on its way to either Sydney or Melbourne, but the fellows on board were desperate to get ashore. Well the first I knew about it was a radio message to the Port Authorities: 'Dentist required immediately on BP oil tanker anchoring outside three mile limit Port Adelaide.'

He looked round our faces and smiled. 'So, because it was an emergency, the harbour lifeboat service roared into life and got me out to that tanker in minutes. When I got there, I found the Captain on deck with two other officers at the ready and nine crew members in a line. Nine crew members! And I extracted a tooth from each of them.'

Then he began laughing so much he had to hold on to the bar to steady himself. 'I pulled a tooth out of each of those nine seamen and there wasn't a squeak out of any of them. Not as much as one squeak out of any of them! And I had only taken enough anaesthetic for two!'

TWO SHIPS

Some of us wonder why office personnel seldom visit company's ships even when they come into a home port. Or if they do come on board, it's a brief business visit to the Captain and a lesser one to the Chief Engineer. They bring some papers requiring signatures and leave, never to be seen again.

I joined the MV 'Ardmore' in London, 'talked shop' with the Second I had come to relieve and then he gave me a guided tour round his engine room.

That engine room was a joy to behold, an immaculate palace of marine technology where every item was polished, painted and gleaming. It looked as if the main engine, boilers and the auxiliaries were brand new, had only been installed that week and had never been used, yet I knew the 'Ardmore' was more than eleven years old.

The Chinese Number One, the head man of the greasers, donkeymen and wipers, came forward and offered each of us a piece of white cloth that wouldn't have been out of place on a dining room table. He remained unobtrusively behind us until I had finally seen everything I had wanted to see and was ready to go up top again.

I signalled to him to come to us. 'You speak English, Number One?'

He nodded. 'I learn some piece all the time.'

'Good. Engine room is beautiful. You do good job.'

He grew two inches taller at my words and his face glowed with pride.

The remainder of the engine room staff were two Chinese Third Engineers, two Chinese Fourth Engineers, two Chinese fitters and a young, highly qualified Chinese

Electrician. The Chief and I were British, and we would cheerfully have sailed in anything that floated.

We left for Hong Kong, a non-stop voyage where everything ran smoothly and sweetly and it was difficult to find things to do that could pass the time. The quality of engineering perfection was maintained.

Then I made a blunder.

Number One had the paint brushes and paint tins out. He intended to put another coat of white gloss on the underside of the engine room skylight and asked for my approval. He held up one of the tins of white gloss. 'This one white paint not good one paint. Two months more, this one paint go brown colour.'

I pondered this. 'Number One, maybe mix little piece blue paint in white paint? Maybe not go brown colour. Just little piece blue.'

That day he had rigged stagings up before lunch and the whole engine room skylight was painted the brightest of blues by the time I took over my watch at four o'clock. When I opened the engine room door, I got a metaphorical wallop from the bright blue haze that shone down on me.

It had quite an impact on Chief Engineer Bill Higgins too, when he saw it. He beamed at me. 'I like it!' he cried. 'I like it!'

When we dropped the anchor in Hong Kong, one of our company's top office staff, Mr Tommy Anderson, came on board to see the Captain and leave a few documents.

The Chief and I pounced on him as he tried to leave the ship and herded him to the engine room door as two collie dogs would with a stray sheep. 'Just a brief look, Mr Anderson, won't keep you a moment. We know you'll be pleased……A bit unusual, perhaps…..'

So Tommy Anderson saw the 'Ardmore' engine room from inside the top engine room door. Then, without any persuasion from the Chief or me, he made a complete tour all the way down to the bottom plates.

It was the absolute cleanliness that amazed him. 'I never thought engine rooms could be anything like this,' he murmured.

When we went back up top his white tropical gear had touches of sweat but he didn't notice. He turned to face both of us thoughtfully. 'My sister and her husband are visiting us just now. Can I bring them and my wife down to let them see your engine room, say, about seven o'clock this evening?'

So, it was agreed, we had four visitors who saw the engine room and were spell bound. But all the credit must go to my predecessor, the Second Engineer I relieved in London and whose name I regret I can't remember. I do hope he reads this.

Again, maybe the impact of a bright blue engine room skylight had something to do with it....

-0-0-0-

I left the 'Ardmore' after eighteen months, had four months paid leave and was requested to join the latest addition to our fleet in Immingham in July, 1964. She was to be called the MV 'Ardtara.' I think the name 'Ardtara' was being slapped on her bow and her rear end when I joined.

She was a British ship with British personnel, most of them had walked off and I noticed some of our Chinese Officers and crew were already on board.

The engine room contained a huge monstrosity of a seven cylinder B&W four stroke, probably the last of her kind, and the engine room itself was little more than a massive rust-ridden scrap yard. There were two boilers, a

Cochran and a Deutch Werft water tube with lots of tubes missing and evidence of other tubes leaking. The wailing of the boiler feed pumps could be heard on the jetty and the slow heavy bumps of the main sea water cooling pump echo-ed through the ship. There were two diesel generators, but the stand-by one had a rocker arm missing and there was no spare. The sump was full of sludge and seawater.

It was quite a nice day weather-wise when I encountered three of her engineers out on deck with their luggage and they were not happy.

We looked at each other for a moment before I spoke. 'OK, lads, who's the Second?'

It was a few moments before anyone answered. 'He's with the Super in the Chief's cabin.' The speaker was a typical 'professional Third', an uncertificated engineer with many years of practical experience but no written qualifications.

'What kind of trip did you have?'

'I'll tell you what kind of trip we had.' He raised his voice and snarled through clenched teeth to spit out every blasphemous swear word that had ever been printed in the English language.

Evidently it had not been a good trip.

Then there were voices coming from the accommodation and a boy came out on deck followed by 'someone from the office.' The boy proved to be the Second Engineer and he came straight to me.

'No stores, no spares, no tools – bugger all!' He screamed. 'They couldn't even supply us with grinding paste to grind in the main engine exhaust valves. The Chief sold the outboard engine off the jolly boat to buy us grinding paste and some stores from garages ashore in Baltimore – we were down to our last tin and it was useless fine stuff. No rags, no cotton waste, no – no steam jointing, no- no……..' But words choked him

The 'someone from the office' appeared out of the accommodation and smiled weakly at us. 'Well, gentlemen, times are hard and we have to do the best we can in those trying times.' He held his brief case in front of his body like a shield and backed off, still talking to placate the group of engineers before him. Their taxis arrived and I never watched such a dejected bunch of seafarers leave a ship in my life.

This ship was now our company's latest acquisition and they must have got it for a song.

The Chief Engineer was Mr Al Savage and I am happy to say he was an expert on dirty big seven cylinder four stroke B&W diesel engines. He and I rapidly became pals.

'Bob, leave it. Let the Third be duty engineer tonight. We are sailing at noon tomorrow. Our Mate is in a taxi going round garages buying grinding paste. Let's give the main engine a kick over before breakfast to make sure she will start OK.' He smiled. 'And if she starts, we sail to Sicily, according to the Captain.'

'And if she doesn't start?'

But Al laughed. 'We'll make her start.'

We gave her a kick before breakfast next morning and she wouldn't start. We gave her a lot of kicks and she still wouldn't start. It was 5.00 pm, nine long hours later, before we coaxed her to fire on one cylinder. We kept her turning on one cylinder until another cylinder started to fire and amid the crashing and banging and the fumes a few other cylinders joined the havoc and chaos until she was erratically ticking over on nearly all seven.

Al grabbed the phone. 'CAST OFF!!' He roared and our damned 'Ardtara' began shuffling its way to Sicily.

We had nine stops on the journey, overhauling exhaust valves, stopping the main engine, fitting two overhauled exhaust valves and grinding in the ones we took out. We worked on pumps, generators, spare main engine fuel valves until we didn't know if it was night time or day time in the world outside the engine room. We slaved and sometimes fell asleep on the job in the smoky atmosphere and the punishing heat.

I never mention our ship owner's name because he and his family were wonderful to all of us and quite new to the world of the shipping.

In Sicily, a new highly qualified superintendent engineer walked on board, saw the Chief and I and told us that he was taking over the engine room for the week end. We, in turn, were ordered, quote, 'to get our backsides ashore and don't come near the engine room until Monday. Orders from the top, just sign for anything you buy.'

Chief Engineer Al Savage, Chief Mate Bill Court, Second Mate Brian St John Early, Sparky?, two deck cadets and I, Bob Jackman made our way round the bars, etc, slept soundly in hotels and finally returned to the MV 'Ardtara' in time for breakfast. I recall each of us carrying a one and a half gallon barrel of local Marsala wine. All bills paid by the local shipping agents to be refunded by our ship owner.

Our highly qualified superintendent engineer, who was proving to be a bit of a superman, had made out his report for the company. He read it out to us and left.

Three days later we set out for Port Said and the Suez Canal. Even before we reached Port Said the heat in the engine room was overpowering. There were four natural draught air vents, no branch vents and consequently we had to hold a rag in our hand before touching anything. Handrails in the top of the engine room could not be held and a spanner laid on the floor plates for a few minutes became too hot to pick up. We were like slaves in Dante's Inferno and breathed the hot fumes with our mouths wide open.

We sailed for Hong Kong and though main engine and the auxiliaries rattled and clattered every inch of the way, we now had no major stops.

Hui Ying of Kai Tak Drydock and Engineering Company was on board before the anchors hit the water and he had four brand new force draught vent fans waiting for us in his work shops. He also had a great pile of stores, spares, boxes of grinding paste and a large squad of experienced fitters.

They were two different ships, two different companies and two different worlds. That was life in some ships in the Merchant Navy in the mid 1960's.

THE JUNIOR'S PROGRESS

Like many others, I have always believed that Chief Engineers should stay out of the engine room unless requested by the Second. A Chief and Second both running the ship's engine room is like having two men in the driving seat of a double decker bus in heavy traffic. Good Chiefs are only there if the Second needs advice or assistance and many Chiefs and Seconds I have sailed with think this way also. Provided, of course, both know their jobs which was not always the case.

I joined the good ship 'MV City of Poona' on a Sunday afternoon. I had been Second Engineer for more than two years and apart from my first five months with a neurotic idiot, I loved every minute of it. On the 'Poona' the Second I was relieving had his bags packed and trying to communicate with him was like trying to hold a conversation with a transistor radio on full volume. Minutes after meeting, he was off and away.

The ship was quiet, it was Sunday and I surmised most of the lads would be ashore. No sign of the duty engineer, so I slipped into my new boiler suit, had a walk round the engine room and found it was a mess.

Up top again, back in uniform, knocked on the Chief's door, no answer, so I made my way to the Officers Smoke Room.

I found five crew members there, three behind the bar, two at the bar. The three behind the bar were the Chief, the Fourth and the Electrician, with their heads inside the bar's refrigerator.

The Chief stood up, looked at me and ignored my introductory stretched out hand, scowled and returned to fiddling with the refrigerator's electrical intestines.

‘Right Fourth, switch it on.’

The Fourth obliged, the refrigerator gave one little ‘Ping’ then fell into an absolute silence again.

‘Switch the bliddy thing off,’ he snarled. ‘We’ll try again tomorrow.’

He then wiped his hands and left the smoke room without a backward glance. The exasperated Lecky and Fourth shook their heads apologetically and they left too. Most of my Chiefs were great men, highly competent engineers and good friends that I could look forward to sailing with again. This wasn’t one of them.

I found the two characters sitting at the bar were the Second Mate, Brian St John Early, and a bright little first trip Seventh Engineer, Gerard O’Hare.

‘They won’t let us use the pantry fridge,’ Brian informed me. ‘Captain’s orders. We’ve had warm beer for nearly a week now.’

I sighed. ‘Tell me, gentlemen, did the refrigerator go ‘ping’ when they switched on?’

They looked at each other, bewildered and answered ‘Yes.’

‘Well, Mister Gerard O’Hare, would you be so kind as to go into the pantry or the galley and bring us a couple of ice trays with ice cubes therein?’

When Gerry returned from the pantry he was carrying two trays of ice cubes.

‘Aha! Clever laddie. Now make your merry way behind the bar put the ice cube trays into the freezer box in the refrigerator. That’s it. Now close the freezer box, shut the refrigerator door and switch on.’

Gerry solemnly went behind the bar, carried out my instructions under our supervision and the refrigerator went ‘ping.’ A long three minutes later it went ‘ping’ again, one minute after that, another ‘ping’ then more ‘pings’ that soon faded to become a quiet purring sound.

We three smiled warmly at each other, comforting smiles of satisfaction at our achieved success.

‘When did the fridge go wrong, Brian?’

‘Er, Tuesday, Bob. The ice box was choked solid with ice and the Second started to de-frost it. Then the Chief intervened and they had a shouting match so the Second left it to him. The Chief has been working on it since then.’ His eyes turned to the refrigerator and he gave a contented smile. ‘I’ve got a cat at home that purrs like that.’

The ice box was performing nicely when the dinner gong sounded so we trouped along to the dining saloon. We three were the first there and we knew our places at the tables. The Chief arrived and though I was sitting at his elbow at the table, he still didn’t even acknowledge my existence. The pig had no manners. To him, I was the invisible man. No wonder my predecessor was eager to leave.

A few others arrived, sat down, and then finally the immaculate Captain Gilchrist entered. The Chief scowled and his eyes briefly flicked sideways at one of the noblest of sea captains in the company.

The silence was deafening.

In a sweet saccharin voice, the Captain asked: ‘Is the officers smoke room refrigerator working yet, Chief? How long has it been off? Tuesday, was it?’

‘She is bliddy well clapped out. It must be quite a good age and the guts just wear so much, there’s nothing much anyone can do with it. You’ll just need to buy a new one before we sail. See the agent. There’s nothing ship staff can do with it. I’ve had this problem before on other ships……..’

‘Ah! You are Mister Jackman?’ Captain Gilchrist interrupted the Chief’s flow of garbage then raised his eye brows and turned to me: ‘Our new Second Engineer Officer. And Mister Gerard O’Hare, Seventh Engineer Officer? Welcome on board, gentlemen. I do hope you like warm beer. You will just have to get used to it. The Chief has been working on the refrigerator all week,’ he added dryly, ‘and achieved nothing.’

Hooray! What a gentleman he was! I liked the man.

‘The refrigerator is working very well, Captain.’ I smiled. ‘Mr O’Hare put it right then started it up before we came up for dinner. Only took three minutes and it is icing up quite nicely.’

The dining saloon atmosphere crackled like static electricity.

‘What was wrong with it, Mister O’Hare?’ The Captain’s eyes widened as he looked at Gerry. They all looked at Gerry.

I answered for him because he was still in awe of his fellow officers and his surroundings. ‘There was nothing wrong with it, Captain. Just the Chief didn’t know how to start it properly.’

I make no apologies for my actions. This ignoramus was no doubt responsible for the engine room being in a mess and had a reputation for spreading gloom and misery among ship staff.

It grieves me to say that he and I never came to blows.

So the days passed, no murders were committed and the Chief lasted a few weeks more before his time with Ellerman’s City Line came to an end. I think he joined Scottish Ship Management.

His successor was an Indian gentleman called Pascal and Mister Pascal was a pleasure to have on board. As the weeks went by, the engine room was put into good order and everything now ran smoothly and sweetly. The smoke room refrigerator ran sweetest of all and it was always full of nice cold beer.

If junior engineers were studying for their qualifications in thermo-dynamics, electro-technology, refrigeration, naval architecture, engineering drawing, higher mathematics, sciences of latent heat, specific heat etc Blah! Blah! Blah! I often gave them some assistance.

Gerry spent all his spare time with his books and I gave him time off to allow him to study. I carried five A4 science note books with me on most ships I joined as Second, five note books with all my notes on the lessons I learned, all practical knowledge not usually found in normal marine text books.

Wee Gerry absorbed every word I taught him. Months afterwards I learned later he passed his Second's Ticket, or the Board of Trade Certificate Second Class Marine Engineering (Motor) to give it its proper title and then continued on his merry way a few years later to Glasgow University to achieve a BSc Engineering (with Honours).

With his wife Betty and three children to provide for, he applied for jobs in his native Glasgow and surrounding areas to no avail. He also applied further south in the north of England but, as in Glasgow, salaries offered were pathetically low.

One company in Manchester sounded promising so he travelled there by train and met one of the managers, to be told, quote: 'Our personnel director didn't come in today. Could you come back to-morrow?'

A very dejected Gerry O'Hare returned to Glasgow.

He had received three letters from America offering a position but he had tossed them aside and the children had torn them to get the American postage stamps.

Then one night the telephone rang. 'I is calling you, Mr O'Hare and I knows you sure has good qualifications. We want you to come and look over what we has to offer. You have family? Great! Bring them with you. We got our Mister Koraz who will call on you and escort you all the way right to our door step. All expenses will be paid, you won't need to put your hands near your pockets at all and I sure means it.'

Two weeks later Gerry, Betty and the three kids were in America and Gerry had become a very important person in a firm that did, quote; 'Advanced Marine Engine Designs', in Newport News, South East Virginia, United States of America.

Some years later, he and Bette returned to Glasgow for a family meeting, then hired a car and raced all the way up to Scotland to Kingussie to pay a visit to my Mary and me. But Mary and I were at sea for a spell so, regretfully, we didn't meet again.

Well, dear pal Gerry O'Hare, you've gone a long way since the day you fixed the refrigerator on the 'City of Poona'.

Cheers, Gerry and Betty, a thousand best wishes to you and the kids. God bless you.

YOKKAICHI

The good ship 'M.V. City of Swansea' carried seven engineers, three mates, three deck cadets, one Captain and a Chief Engineer. Seven of us were in our mid-twenties or less and we had sailed from Newcastle in England to Yokkaichi in Japan with one brief stop for bunkers. It was a long trip that took a long time before we were finally dropped the anchor off the Japanese coast. Ten days went by before we moved alongside the port's only berth.

The year was 1957. I was an ageing twenty-seven and being the oldest going ashore that night I felt responsible for the innocents of twenty-six years and under who had never been to Japan before.

But Yokkaichi was unknown to any of us and no more than a tiny spot behind a little known Japanese island and a far distance from the Utopian ports of Yokohama, Kobe, Osaka and others. Our youngsters were eager to get their feet on dry land for a while, land that abounded with pretty girls and cold beer and more pretty girls.

All seven of us trouped ashore into a crowded world where few locals had seen Europeans before. The pedestrians we passed on the streets looked at us in amazement, said 'Hi' and nodded. So we said 'Hi' to them and nodded and this caused a lot of amusement to all.

Another ancient Japanese custom is in saying 'thank you' when they are extremely grateful for something you have done. The males bow, place the tips of their fingers on their foreheads and say, 'domo arigato'. Japanese ladies kiss the palms of the hands of the person they are so grateful to. They also say 'domo arigato.' The person being thanked replies with 'doi tasha masti.' ('Thank you' and 'Don't mention it' respectively)

We found long vertical banners displaying Japanese characters were hanging outside every building. None of them, however, could inform us that they were a place for our requirements, our requirements being local ladies and local beer in that order.

Then, suddenly, down a narrow side street, among all the vertical, multicoloured banners, we spotted one banner that said 'The Red Lion'! We ventured forth at speed and entered.

Many of the hostelries in the Far East are run with one mature manageress and a few girls to serve customers in any way the customers wished to be served. There were four men at a table imbibing a local brew when we arrived and all heads turned to look at us.

We shouted 'Hi!' to them and nodded our heads, they shouted 'Hi!' to us, nodded their heads and everyone was overjoyed.

Then a girl of outstanding beauty approached us. 'Would you like to sit here?'

She could speak English! And we were all fascinated by this beauty. It wasn't the kind of beauty that was painted on a face in the morning and washed off at night; she was just naturally a very beautiful creature, a beauty and grace that Nature had bestowed on her in abundance.

'Seven beers, please.'

'Please. You like Kirin, Asahi or Sapporo beers?'

'Kirin, please.'

My associates were still drooling as she returned with the beers. They watched her every movement and she was becoming quite aware of their thoughts. When she blushed their drooling increased.

'Where can my friends meet some nice friendly girls?' I asked.

Her fingers touched her cheek to cover her embarrassment. 'You speak your friends go down this street. They come to big street. In big street, they will find girls for rent in shop windows. Shop girls all good health. Do not take girls from street.' She waved a finger at us for emphasis. 'Not from street.'

I never saw beers downed so quickly and my fellow companions were off, racing down the street without a 'Good-bye or see you soon.'

She was taking the empties from the table when she whispered. 'Please, I am not for rent. I do not do sex. Maybe you should go with your friends.'

Her closeness was causing tightness in my chest. 'When you want me to go, I will go. I am happy you are not for rent. But tell me, where did you learn English?'

She stood with the tray of empties in her hands, her teeth nibbling her lip. 'Take books from library. Some books I buy. My mother she speak my father was Scottish man.'

'I am Scottish.'

Her eyes widened. 'Is true this thing?'

I nodded.

Then she left me to serve the old man sitting alone in the corner, now her last remaining customer. After serving him she returned to me. 'Old man like speak with you. You not angry?' she whispered.

I turned round in my chair and gave him a pantomime salute. 'Bring us two beers,' I whispered. 'I like to speak with old man.'

There were only the three of us left in the bar so she came and sat with us, interpreted everything we said and served us with the beers as required. We laughed a lot, had more beers and eventually the old man's head began to droop and he fell asleep.

I sighed. 'Lassie, call a taxi. We'll take him home.'

So a taxi was called, we three sat in the back and saw the old chap safely home. He lived in a wooden house in Yokkaichi's little dock area and on our return to the Red Lion we were passing close to my good ship, 'City of Swansea.' It was a beautiful night, the moon was out and I squeezed her hand in mine.

I whispered. 'That's my ship. Shall we stop?'

She didn't answer but the driver must have known the English word 'stop', so he stopped and waited. I could nearly hear her heart beating. I paid the driver and escorted her up the ship's gangway to my cabin. The only sound was the gentle purring of the diesel generator far below in the engine room. She was nervous and apprehensive.

We entered the cabin quietly; I locked the door and gently took her in my arms. She buried her face in my neck for a few moments then looked up into my eyes. We kissed gently. I guided her hand down to the bulge in the front of my trousers, felt her sharp intake of breath and saw the startled look in her eyes. Many minutes later we undressed slowly and climbed up into my bunk. When she stopped trembling we started having sex but I was finding it difficult.

'You are too much big,' she moaned.

Then suddenly I was not 'too much big.' Neither was I 'too much big' in the hours that followed.

Dawn was breaking when we walked down the deserted streets, hand in hand, back to 'The Red Lion.' We stopped outside the bar and gazed lovingly at each other. Then she took both my hands, kissed the palms softly and looked at me.

'Domo arigato,' she whispered.

'Doi tasha masti,' I replied.

There were tears in her eyes, but there were stars in them too.

SEX IN KUPANG

The need for sex can be as demanding as the need for food but whereas, with hunger, the male of our species can request food from any man or woman and eat almost anything given, protocol does not permit the male to openly request sex from a lady. But many a true lady that can secretly and willingly satisfy a good man's sexual needs is fondly remembered and loved by that man for many years.

We met in with some fellow seafarers from another ship in one of the Flying Angel Seamen's Clubs out in the Far East somewhere, the beer flowed and everybody had a tale to tell.

We had the usual cry: 'Shall we talk about sex or just wait until it crops up?' and, of course, it did crop up after the second beer.

Then Lecky began with a story. 'I remember a good Fifth Engineer called Willie Baines, a young lad, and dead keen on the job. We were heading for a place called Kupang in Indonesia after a long bliddy haul for months up and down the China Coast when we got a bad leak on a steam valve. So Willie being Willie, he got a couple of spanners out to tighten it up but the whole bliddy gland blew out on him, right on to his face. Well, on his neck, mostly, and on his hands as he tried to save his face.'

'Were you far from port?' I asked. In cases like this on board any ship, all you can offer is sympathy and bandages.

'It was two days before we reached Kupang and there was an ambulance waiting for us when we arrived. Well, to make a long story longer, four of us went to the hospital later that day to see him. Hospital? It was a conglomeration…'

‘What’s a conglomeration?’ Danny, deck cadet was not the brightest member of our group.

‘It was a bliddy big assortment of wooden sheds and huts all nailed together and the mozzies rose in great clouds everywhere: mozzies and creepy-crawlies. We went visiting after the medical staff had a chance to bandage him up a bit and we found he had a wee shed all to himself and a single bed inside a kind of tent of mosquito netting. He had so much wadding and bandages wrapped round his neck we thought it was a pillow they had stuck under his chin. Again, his two hands looked as if he was wearing a big pair of white boxing gloves. Poor bastard.’

‘Was he in any pain?’

‘He was in bliddy agony when he moved his head or his arms, but he always had a nurse in the hut with him. Nurses took turns looking after him. There was one…….’

Then Lecky stopped there and moved his bottle of beer in circles on the table for a few moments while we silently waited for him to continue.

Then he went on: ‘I don’t know if I should go on with this story. But it’s all true, honestly.’

‘Then tell it!’

‘True stories are always the best stories.’

There were other calls of encouragement from the six of us. Our group had grown and now six more bottles of ice cold beer had appeared.

‘Come on, don’t stop there, Lecky.’

‘Well,’ he went on, ‘as I said, he always had a nurse with him, an Indonesian nurse, a different one every few hours and they attended to him.’

‘Female?’

‘Aye. And if he needed the loo?’

‘The nurses just got help from a couple of male nurses. But communicating was difficult because none of the nurses could speak a word of English and Willie was in agony all the time. He couldn't move his head because the front of his neck was raw scalded flesh that had gone brittle in places. It was like one great patch of raw flesh. Christ! It must have been bliddy agony for him.'

Our group was increased when two more MN types joined us and the quantity of beer being consumed was assisting conversation.

'Let me tell you something about native women. Native women in places like Indonesia are more female than our women back home. They have a different way of looking at things. You know; things like sex. Sex is a hunger, just like needing something to eat. Try dangling a big pork pie in front of a starving man and you'll see what I mean.'

'Well, we know what it's like. Don't stop there.'

There were a few more encouraging comments, requesting Lecky to continue.

'Well, just picture it. It was hot in that shed. He was covered from the waist down in a single white sheet, unable to move, inside a tent made of mosquito netting and his every movement was watched by a young, attractive Indonesian nurse. She was the one who washed the sweat from his upper half carefully avoiding going too close to his neck. His eyes and her eyes were saying all that needed to be said when she lowered the sheet covering the lower half of his naked body and gently washed his legs, feet, penis and testicles in that order.' Then he repeated: 'Legs, feet, penis and testicles in that order. Next morning when she washed him he came in her washing cloth.'

'He *came?'*

'Aye, he came. He had an orgasm that exhausted him as if he had just run a four minute mile.'

The room was quiet and the lads looked at each other without a word being said. The bottoms of the empty beer glasses were being closely examined.

Suddenly the bartender approached with a tray carrying ten bottles of beer. 'I've been listening to every bliddy word you lot said. Right! Here's a beer for each of you, that's nine, one for me, makes ten and they are all on the house if I can park my backside with you.'

Who could refuse the good man's generosity? We approved and moved the chairs around to make room for him.

Lecky nibbled his lower lip for a moment and his voice was a bit quieter. 'It was nearly a week before a doctor, a Dutchman, appeared to examine Willie. He came from a town on one of the larger islands and informed Willie that he would be moved to a hospital in Jakarta in about ten days time. It wouldn't be practical to move him before that.'

His voice had gone quieter. He coughed to clear his throat.

'Willie and his nurse grew even more passionate in their love making and from quietly masturbating she changed to giving him oral sex. It was the day before he was due to leave for Jakarta that she removed all her clothes and squatted on him, straddling him so he entered deep into her and had a massive climax.' Lecky then took a long swallow of his beer and focussed his eyes on the bottle's label. 'Don't know what happened to Willie after he left Kupang.'

The bartender looked round all of us. 'Well, I'll tell you what happened to your Willie. It's Willie Thomson you're talking about. Well Willie had a whole five weeks in Jakarta and his shipping company flew him back to the UK for plastic surgery. After a long spell in the

Dreadnought Hospital in London getting his neck patched up, he quit the Merchant Navy and came back out to Indonesia to marry his nurse, but she didn't recognise him. She didn't even want to know him. She had hurriedly married an Indonesian bloke because Willie had had got her pregnant. Well, Willie was heart broken but eventually he married a teacher in Jakarta who taught English and he got himself a job teaching English to Indonesians as well. How do I know this? His wife who also taught English was the one that taught me how to speak Indonesian years ago.'

He moved his chair back and started to gather up the empties. 'Well, I couldn't run a bliddy pub if I couldn't communicate with the locals, could I?'

GONE TO BLAZES

There comes a time in every seaman's life when he has to retire from deep sea shipping and doesn't know how to fit in the shore side life. I have heard of ex-Captains, ex-Chiefs and others who ended up sitting at home, watching telly, getting in the way of their relatives and talking to the wallpaper. But what can they do when they retire?

When the village tourist season was over, I found myself assisting in the local drama club. Long spells of sailing all over the world were now over and better left to younger men. I did have an occasional week or two in the coastal trade, when required. Like the time a diving ship in Grimsby needed a Chief Engineer for forty-eight hours so I jumped into my car and drove the 390 miles from Kingussie in Invernesshire to Grimsby.

The Captain awaited me on deck. 'Ah! So sorree, Meester Jackman, our Chief Engineer he arrive all right, pleez.' He handed me an envelope. 'There be £200 in envelope – railways are so much expensive these days.'

'But that's my car at the gangway. I drove down here.'

'Sorry, but I not see any one car at the gangway,' he shrugged his shoulders, smiled and turned away.

Still, £200 was one good day's work and there were others.

Playing darts in a village pub was so much easier than playing on a ship, particularly on a ship that seemed to wobble a lot when I needed a double to finish and there was a round of beers at stake.

But my claim to fame on the dartboard happened when I had been married a couple of weeks. I felt like having a beer so I took a stroll down to the bar in the Duke of Gordon hotel and met one of Kingussie's brightest stars,

Hughie Tort. He was alone and leaning over his pint. Beside him on the bar was a new set of darts, still in their plastic wrapper.

'You're Mary Carmichael's husband?'

'Well, Mary Carmichael is my wife.'

'Can you play darts?'

'Aye, I can play darts.'

'We always play for a whisky here.'

'Good.'

There is a time in every man's life when the whole world is on his side and his darts don't miss. This was one such rare occasion and it was a star studded evening for me. Other members of the Duke of Gordon's Dart Team arrived, took me on and I won every game I played.

Eventually, it was closing time and I was now 'Bob' to all other players. Then the surprise hit me.

'C'mon, Bob, drink up. These whiskies on the table are yours.'

I hadn't realised that the loser in each game had to put a whisky up for the winner on the table and I hadn't lost a game. There were eight whiskies on the table.

'Give me a hand with them, lads?'

Eight voices in unison bawled 'No!' and each face watched mine.

So I raised the first glass and poured the whisky into my mouth and smiled. Then I raised my pint beer glass, not to drink the beer but to dribble the whisky in my mouth into it. I did this eight more times, left my pint beer glass which was now 90% whisky and had another whisky at the bar.

But there's another side to this story that didn't come to light until long after the bar closed.

Auld Wullie, gentleman bartender of many years standing, would never have a drink when serving. At the end of the day, after he had locked up, he would collect all the dirty glasses and drink the contents of each before washing them. Not many dishes were washed that night. He had flaked out behind the bar and was still lying there at six o'clock the following morning.

My heart was still in the Merchant Navy and it always will be, but I was adapting to village life, a Scottish Highland village life where everyone is a friend.

There were still times I was called upon to 'stand by' a ship or take one over for a couple of weeks, but generally my life was settling into the village and the villagers.

I was finishing my second or sixth pint of the evening when Jimmy Murchie called; 'Hey, Bob! Would you like to join the Fire Brigade?'

'Do I need to be brave?'

'No, you don't need to be brave.'

'OK. I'll join your Fire Brigade.'

So a short time passed and I had become a member of the Fire Brigade, Duke of Gordon Darts Team and the Drama Club. I did not intend to suffer the acute loneliness of old retired seafarers that live in solitude with 'Coronation Street.'

Jimmy had been the leader of Kingussie Fire Brigade for many years and was a hero to all in that area of the Cairngorms. In fact, they were all heroes.

My first lesson on fire fighting was when an upstairs bedroom in one of the old houses in the village went on fire. Evidently the occupier's son had been imbibing too freely in one of the local pubs, had gone to bed smoking a cigarette and the bed had caught fire.

'Right, Bob, you drag the hose upstairs and put the fire out.'

The hose was already connected to the pump, the valves were open, the pressure was in the line and all I had to do was open the cock.

'Whoopee,' I boldly thought, 'a chance to prove myself! I'll show them what a Merchant Navy engineer can do.'

I dragged the hose upstairs and kicked the door open. The smoke in the room was so thick it looked as if the room was stuffed with cotton wool. I couldn't see, I couldn't breathe and I suddenly found I didn't know what way was up. Someone dragged me backwards down the stairs head first, spread me out face down on the gravel driveway and the others put the fire out.

'Bob, that was your first lesson. Remember this! If there is a fire in an enclosed space like that bedroom, the only place you will find air is at floor level. Air is heavier than warm smoke. Another thing to remember is this: if you have to go into a blazing room, stick close to the walls. The fire can cause the centre of the floor to collapse and you could fall through. OK?'

I learned. That was my first lesson and, like all idiots, I always thought I was so clever. I found in the long hours that followed, I coughed, sneezed and farted smoke rings.

Some months later I had a call from my shipping company to briefly 'stand-by' one of their ships. As in most cases at sea, you can join a ship and find you have excellent squad of engineers on board. Other times you can find a mixture of heroes and half wits. On that particular ship at that particular time, I found few heroes, just half wits and the engine room was a shambles.

The Chief Engineer kept his cabin door locked and informed me, quote, 'he didn't want to get involved.' Where in the hell did the company get him from? What did he not want to get involved in?

My predecessor was a nervous wreck that had to be paid off and I couldn't get any sense out of him. He had been terrorised by the big bully of a Third Engineer so when I met the big bully of a Third Engineer he learned who gave the orders and found it was no longer him.

The Fourth Engineer was a spoiled Mummy's boy who wasn't going to take orders from anyone. He had never obeyed his mummy, why should he obey a total stranger like me? He should have brought his mother along. We probably would have found she was more of an asset to the male ship's staff than her spoiled brat of a son.

We also had three Junior Engineers who were bewildered about who they were to obey. I made everything clear to all at our first meeting and ruthlessly substantiated it at our second.

The old adage: 'A Second Engineer is either a bad bastard or a stupid bastard' rings true. Once your authority is established you can ease up and be friendly. I was a stupid bastard in my first year as Second Engineer that ended with two heart attacks and fourteen days in the Dreadnought Merchant Navy Hospital.

It was that way only once.

One of the many faults I found on that first day was three acetylene and three oxygen bottles tied up in a corner of the engine room workshop. The hoses lay tangled on top of the bottles and the acetylene torch looked a bit battered and twisted. A confusion of rope and wire slings, chain blocks and other lifting gear shared the corner with the gas bottles.

A blue boiler-suited hard man appeared at my elbow. He looked as if he was in his forties so I correctly guessed he was engine room Storekeeper. No introductions were necessary.

‘Stores, I want you to take two oxygen and two acetylene bottles up to the after deck and tie them to the ship’s rail. Leave a full one of each down here.’

Stores sucked his teeth for a moment and then nodded. Just at that moment the big Third Engineer Who Shall Remain Nameless strolled into the workshop. My mind went back momentarily to some of the great Thirds I had sailed with in the past and thought how I missed them. Then I had a long look at this surly brute.

‘The Captain and the Chief are in the control room,’ he informed me, disdainfully. ‘I think they want to talk to you.’

‘Do you keep a workbook on the work you have done on the generators? Right, I want to see it today. Just make sure it’s up to date.’

I pushed past him and left him staring after me.

The control room was an enclosed area with windows that looked out to the main engine, a six cylinder Doxford. For those that don’t know what a six cylinder Doxford looks like, it’s an engine that stands three decks high and is well over forty foot long.

On that side of the control room was the main panel with its grand array of gauges, switches and little coloured lights. On the outboard wall was the main electrical switchboard with its voltmeters, ammeters, rows of breakers, switches and fuses, a galaxy of electrical complexities that controlled everything of that nature on board ship.

I entered and the Captain moved forward to meet me; the Chief Engineer stayed where he was and scowled. He looked surly, like a naughty child that had just been smacked by mummy.

‘Ah, Mister Jackman? I’m Captain Charles Lorrimer.’ (A Captain assisting in an engine room!) We shook hands and the Chief's scowl deepened. 'The Company have sent a circular round all the ships requesting information on equipment on board for fire fighting. The Chief tells me he ordered a ten gallon foam extinguisher for the control room and we were discussing where we would put it.'

I could have told them where to put it, but refrained.

'Captain? This switchboard is made of mild steel, copper, brass, and glass, materials that are non-inflammable. In the event of anything overheating or over-loading, fuses would blow, breakers would jump out and other safety devices would come into play without any damage being done. You might get some cable insulation burning but even that is most unlikely. To use a foam fire extinguisher on a live switchboard could electrocute the idiot using it.'

It was at that moment that Stores and two of his men went past, hauling one of the gas bottles up the engine room ladders.

The Captain raised his eyebrows a few millimetres and looked at me without speaking.

'Six oxy-acetylene bottles in the work shop, Captain. I am having four of them put out on deck, tied to the shipside rails. If there is ever a fire with the acetylene I want it to be up top on the open deck in the fresh air, not in the confined space of the engine room workshop.'

He looked at the Chief who examined his finger nails and said nothing, then looked at me and nodded his approval. I think Captain Lorrimer and I would get on well together. So far, he was the first one who knew his job. Bless you, Charles Lorrimer, I needed you.

I little thought that these same oxy-acetylene bottles would be one of the most frightening events in my years at sea. Eight days later, it came to pass, it came to pass.

The Fourth had been warned not to use the oxy-acetylene equipment unless either the Third or I was there with him. But it still happened when we were berthed somewhere in the Thames.

'FIRE!'

The Fourth had burned through a heavy steel bar and the hot chunk of steel had dropped on to the acetylene hose, cutting it. It ignited, rapidly burned away the hose and the huge flame was now roaring out of the top of the acetylene bottle when Stores and I got there. The fire pump was situated on the bottom plates with its valves always open and its starter button was in the engineers' alleyway. We connected the fire hose within seconds and I directed the powerful jet of water straight at the valve on top of the bottle. It shut off the flame though the gas still roared out. Had the water jet hit the bottle, the flame and air would have been sucked into the bottle and the explosion would have splattered us into big red patches all over the workshop.

We continued to hose down the burning paintwork on the bulkheads, the air was stinking but becoming breathable and some of the others were warily coming down the main entrances. Stores and I went up on deck, gasping for clean air and left them to get on with it.

The Mate was still safely on deck, dragging hoses and extinguishing apparatus out of a box he had found in a deck storeroom. Stores and I staggered to the shipside rail and stood wheezing great bucketfuls of the pure dockside air into our lungs. Suddenly he turned, took my hand and shook it firmly without saying a word. Bless you Captain Charles Lorrimer, bless you Stores, but where in the Hell did that shipping company get the others from?

SCOURIE HOTEL

Being retired from the Merchant Navy does have its moments when you make yourself available to the coastal trade and similar pastimes. Your name and qualifications become known to the right people, the telephone rings and you find yourself are on the next train to your next job where there are ships.

For instance: 'Ah, yes, Mister Jackman? We would like you to be there when we test run a new engine fitted on one of our coasters – to be given a six hour run and want your opinion - you'll be picked you up at the Scourie Hotel in Sutherlandshire on Thursday morning at 6.00am – yes! - we've booked a room for you there. G-bye!'

I have had stranger phone calls than that since high blood pressure meant I was no longer suitable for sailing to far distant parts. Life became an interesting economic pastime. Most of the jobs were on coasters to the Continent and back or 'standing by' a ship alongside a jetty, but it certainly was an acceptable world for someone used to being an active member of our British Merchant Navy. The money was quite acceptable too and one can get so tired of watching 'Coronation Street' as an alternative.

Scourie Hotel is probably the best of all the good hotels in the north of Bonnie Scotland.

I always remember the words of an old Captain I once sailed with. He said, 'Bob, up there ye can get drunk on the scenery alone, as well as the whisky.'

As soon as I arrived on Wednesday evening and given a lovely room with a view, I naturally made my way to the lounge. I found five couples there who turned and raised their eyes when I ordered a pint of ale and sat myself down at the bar.

In those days, there was no television in the area so the hotel's guests made themselves comfortable in the lounge and talked freely with each other. Everyone was encouraged to tell stories about their lives, where they had been, what they had seen etcetera and newcomers were not allowed to be silent strangers. As always, it was a warm, friendly atmosphere, almost as if they had been close friends for years.

Since I was the latest addition to this cheery band of locals and tourists, I was obliged to introduce myself.

'Well, my name is Bob Jackman, born in Glasgow in 1929, spent forty-one years as an engineer officer in the Merchant Navy, invalided out with high blood pressure and now retired, but I do sometimes get called out for odd jobs with boats or ships around the coast. Sometimes I have brief spells in wonderful hotels like this, all expenses paid and then I'm off home again. Aye, it's a good life for a retired seaman.'

Immediately there were questions about my forty years tramping round the world and what was life in the Merchant Navy like?

The smiling bartender/owner whispered, 'Keep talking, Mr Jackman, and there will be another beer coming when you finish that one.'

It seems I was now promoted to being the centre piece of the merry band.

'Merchant Navy? To begin, in the 1930s, wages were pathetic for officers and crew alike, but it was a job. The Captain was given an allowance to pay for the ship's food in any port they went to, but most of them pocketed a percentage of it then gave some to the Chief Steward. The Chief Steward had his whack of the money, bought the cheapest food stuffs he could find and dumped it on the cook. The cook sold some of it to the dock labourers in any of the foreign ports they went to and quietly pocketed the cash.' I took a long pull at my pint and looked at my audience, hoping someone else would do the talking for a while. 'That was life in the Merchant Navy during the Depression in the 1930s.'

I could see I had their attention and they were not letting go.

So I continued. 'When the war started, life wasn't much better. For instance, if your ship was torpedoed and sank, your pay was stopped until you joined your next ship. Even if you were ten or twenty days in an open lifeboat out in the Atlantic, your wages going home to your wife and family were still stopped from the time your ship was sunk. Your family received nothing from your shipping company because they said you were no longer earning anything for the shipping company. They were pleased to inform you that the lifeboat you were sitting in was supplied by them at no cost to the seamen.'

I looked round their faces. Some were in shock so I hesitated. 'Shall I go on?'

There was a nodding of heads and many cries of 'Yes, please', so I supped more ale and continued.

'Life was difficult indeed if you were in a convoy of ships, and your ship got torpedoed and sunk. You and your mates were now left behind. You could be left sitting in a crowded lifeboat somewhere in the mid-Atlantic, watching all the other ships in the convoy disappearing into the distance. But then a British destroyer would race towards you, going flat out, and ram your lifeboat, cutting it in two. It would then continue back to the convoy leaving a pile of bleeding corpses floating in the Atlantic.'

This made them gasp. ‘Good Gawd! We murdered our own men?’

There were a few similar cries, with male guests clearing their throats and the ladies holding their handkerchiefs to their faces.

‘But why? Why did they murder their own men in the lifeboats?’

I explained quietly. ‘There was always a danger that one of the ships in the convoy would return to pick up the men in the lifeboats. The U-boat that sank your ship could be quietly submerged just under the surface, waiting and using the men in the lifeboat as bait. If a ship did go back, they sank it as well. It did happen, many times.’

One old chap about my age waved his pipe at me to attract my attention. ‘Sir, you would be too young in those days to be a part of all this warfare, so how could you really know all the facts?’

‘In 1950 I joined the Merchant Navy after serving a five year apprenticeship in Barclay Curle’s Engine Works on the Clyde. I was twenty years old then, but some of the old chaps I sailed with in the 1950s had come right through the war and survived. On odd occasions after a few beers, they would recall things that had happened, all that they had seen.’

The owner’s wife came into the lounge and whispered: ‘Telephone call for you, Mr Jackman. You can take it in the office.’

It proved to be the owner of the coaster to inform me that I would be collected at six o’clock in the morning to sail with it down the coast to Oban. I didn’t have to do anything except be on board.

When I informed the owner’s wife she smiled. ‘Our kitchen maid will take your breakfast up to your room at five-thirty. Will porridge, bacon, eggs, toast, orange juice and tea be satisfactory?'

Who could say 'No!' to a breakfast like that?

I returned to the lounge and all eager faces looked at me as I entered. They had moved their armchairs to form a circle with one empty chair for me. My pint glass had been almost empty when I had left to go to the phone and it was now replaced with a full one. I do like Scourie Hotel.

I told them I was to be collected at six o'clock in the morning and I hoped I wouldn't disturb anyone.

'You won't disturb anyone, laddie. No, of course you won't!' It was the old man with the pipe who spoke and they all agreed unanimously.

'Tell us more about the Merchant Navy in the war. About being torpedo-ed and ending up in lifeboats and all that.'

The civilian population in the United Kingdom really knew very little of what the Merchant Navy went through in the war years and the guests were eager to hear more. I just happened to be in the mood to tell them what I had learned.

'In the lifeboats, the seats you sat on were actually cupboards full of emergency food supplies. Many a time the shipwrecked crew opened them when they needed them, to find the food supplies had been stolen by dock labourers.' I repeated it slowly. 'To find the food supplies had been stolen by dock labourers.'

Some of their faces were white with sheer disgust that things like that could happen to men stranded in lifeboats in the open sea.

I looked at them. 'More?'

There were whispers of 'Yes' from all of them.

There are probably lots of people who think these stories should not be told but to be fair to all the men I sailed with for forty years, I believe otherwise.

I swilled the beer around in my glass for a few minutes.

'Oil tankers were the hardest hit. If a U-boat torpedoed an oil tanker, it would explode like a great box of fireworks; the oil would spread over the surface of the sea and ignite and the seamen very often would have no time to lower lifeboats. They would grab a life jacket and leap into the blazing sea. When they came to the surface, they got burnt. If they stayed underwater, they drowned. They soon chose to discard their lifejackets and drown.'

All were quiet for a few minutes then one attractive lady pursed her lips and looked directly at me for a moment. 'You described what happened very well. I would say that you have a gift for telling the public what happened in the war. Why not write the stories down and get them published? I'm sure they would sell well.'

I liked the way she looked at me. I hoped the others didn't notice the way she looked at me.

'Have you ever thought of writing a book about being in the Merchant Navy?'

'I have written a few. Well three, actually.'

This raised their eyebrows. 'You have written three books?'

'Well, four books actually, if you include my book on poetry. I started writing a few years ago on board a ship that had only six European Officers and a crew of thirty Chinese. We were stuck up the China Coast for months, no mail getting in, and no mail getting out. So, I used my writing pads to write stories and the others liked them. It was just something to do and it was better than sitting in my cabin staring at the bulkhead, waiting to go on watch. It became a portfolio of Merchant Navy stories. When I paid off the ship I gave them to an old woman, a widow whose husband had been a book publisher. She called the book 'SHARK' and I told her to keep the profits. Dammit! Well, it is still paying her more than she is getting from her old age pension. My second book is called, 'Merchant Navy Heroes and Half Wits', and it is selling very well. My third book is called 'Merchant Navy. What a Life!' Again, it's a book that is selling well and I am now on Book Four', as yet untitled, but it will give suggestions on what men could do when they retire from the Merchant Navy and get sick of watching telly.'

The evening drew to an end, everybody said nice things about my sea stories and the men shook my hand. Each lady touched her cheek against mine briefly and tenderly and the one very attractive lady did actually kiss my cheek and squeeze my hand tightly as she whispered 'good-night'.

'Sleep well,' she breathed but here eyes said more.

At five-thirty next morning, the little old kitchen maid cheerfully brought me my tray with its full breakfast.

I was already washed and almost completely dressed when the aforementioned very attractive lady suddenly appeared in my doorway, dressed in a very, very short flimsy nightgown and a dressing gown that hung wide open from her shoulders to her toes.

'Oops!' she said when she saw the little old kitchen maid standing behind the door with my breakfast tray. 'Sorry. Wrong cabin.'

Well, we all make mistakes sometimes.

THE BEGINNING OF THE END

When sweet Mary Carmichael and I married, we took a mortgage on a house in her home village of Kingussie in Invernessshire. Since her predecessors and relations had lived in that area for hundreds of years, I knew she would never be too lonely when I was earning our daily bread on the high seas. The villagers were like one family. The whole village soon knew who I was and when I was coming home on leave. A walk down the main street with Mary let me collect a morning newspaper and was punctuated with greetings and hand shakes from the villagers about every ten paces.

Old Grant Menzies was the newsagent on the High Street and he was always quietly eager to know where I had been, what the ship was like and if the officers and crew were good lads. He asked all the questions and it wasn't until a couple of days later did I find that Grant was ex-Merchant Navy, a retired ship's captain no less. Then it was my turn to make him tell me about his life at sea. Soon this developed into having an evening with him at his home while his wife, Lyn, quietly knitted socks for one of the village charities; then Grant began to tell me a few stories about his life in the Merchant Navy in the war years.

He was soft spoken and quite calm when he told me about the horror of the Atlantic convoys. He was Mate on a general cargo ship berthed in New York when the ship's design was altered to make sleeping quarters for seventy American troops.

'However,' he sighed, 'those in authority didn't think to put extra life boats on board. I can talk to you about these things, Bob, because you know what I'm talking about. If I try to tell the locals, I just get blank stares. They are all wonderful people, every one of them, but not a seafarer among them. Lyn and I are from Aberdeen and we may go back there before we get any older.'

Lyn put down her knitting. 'Grant Menzies, you have never told anyone much about your life in the Merchant Navy before. Not even me! I think I'll put the kettle on.' She went smartly off into the kitchen.

Grant eased his old bones out of his armchair and took a bottle of whisky and two glasses from a sideboard. He raised the bottle to eye level for my observation, looked at me and nodded for my approval.

I nodded, he filled two glasses.

When Lyn returned with the tea she stopped abruptly. 'That bottle has aged considerably since the year you bought it, darling, and that was a long time ago.'

Then there was a long silence.

Grant drained his glass and stared into it. Since he had drained his glass, I drained my glass.

'Murmansk,' he said quietly. 'The Murmansk convoys: All that ice and snow and freezing winds.'

I didn't interrupt his silence, and then he went on. 'They mounted two machine guns on the monkey island above the wings of the bridge, one port and one starboard. Then they built a steel box behind each gun, just big enough to store the boxes of ammunition and for a gunner to sit in. Just big enough for a man to *live* in when we got up among the ice. Each box had a tubular kind of electric heater.'

He filled the glasses again but we didn't touch them. His mind had gone back to the days of the Murmansk convoys.

The cups of tea on the tray were going cold and his dear wife Lyn was sitting upright in her armchair, her hands clenched on her lap and her face white.

'Oh, Grant,' she whispered.

I don't think he heard her. 'We were attacked by U-boats. German planes flew overhead and directed the U-boats to where we were and the U-boats just ploughed in and sunk everything around us. Some of us made it to Murmansk. If your ship sank and you ended up in the water you froze to death within minutes.'

He rubbed his face for a moment, and then went on. 'I remember one day when we were being attacked that the boy in the port gun box never fired a shot. When the guns fired on the monkey island the noise on the bridge was deafening so we knew he hadn't fired his gun. We were one of the few ships that made it into Murmansk. Thirty-five ships in the convoy and we lost twenty-four of them. The Captain told me to check how the port gunner was, why he hadn't been firing his gun.' Grant's voice was now a whisper. 'I found the boy was still in his box. His electric heater had fused and he had frozen to death. So we left him there, discharged our cargo and started our journey home. On the morning of the second day, the boy's body was as brittle as a glass statue and we had to use a hammer and chisel to break him into pieces to get him out of the box.'

Lyn's fists were now hard against her mouth and her eyes were wide in horror. Grant got up, put his arms round her and held her tight to control her shaking.

She sobbed. 'Oh, Grant, you have never told me that story before. You've never told me *anything* about your war in the Merchant Navy before.'

'Lyn, I have never told anyone anything about the Murmansk convoys before. But I needed to tell somebody about that one before I go. That's why I'm telling Bob. I've lived with all the details and memories inside me since 1942.'

I knocked back my whisky and put my empty glass on the table. 'Grant, this is a good time for me to go. Ok? I'll see you in the morning. I'll be down for my paper as usual. G'night, Lyn.'

I gave his arm a comforting squeeze and went home.

As the weeks went by, we often had a good crack in the shop about our seafaring days when I was buying my morning paper. Then, as I was leaving, his parting words were, 'I'll sell this shop to you one day, Bob. I'll sell it to you.'

And so it came to pass, that I decided that I was not getting any younger and offered to buy his shop. His price was ridiculously low and he wouldn't raise it.

'Och, Bob, the wife and I have more than enough money to see us out, we have no one to leave it to, and we would like you to have it. When we sell it we can go back to Aberdeen.'

So it came to pass that I became the newsagent in the High Street in Kingussie and Grant and his dear wife sold up their house and went back to their home town of Aberdeen.

The business thrived. Mary and I were enthusiastic; sales increased, I did newspaper deliveries, sold toys and always had a story for the school kids that came to buy sweets. Mary ran the Brownies and I sometimes gave a talk to the Cubs about being in the Merchant Navy. The children just knew me as Bob, the newsagent. When I turned up the first time in Merchant Navy uniform with Second Engineer's gold braid, I will always remember the astonishment on their faces. To them, I was no longer Bob the Newsagent. I was now Mr Jackman, Merchant Navy Officer and I had seen the whole world. I like to think that the cubs realised there was a mighty different world outside the realms of this village they were born in.

Then, when the house next to the shop went vacant, we sold 'Bracken Brae', our detached house on Middle Terrace and bought 'St Arlans.'

I now lived a quiet leisurely life, joined the drama club, played darts in the local and fished for trout in the beautiful River Spey that ran by the village.

Months went by. I was adapting to being a villager, even if I did do short sea trips occasionally, leaving my Mary to run the shop.

My hobby of painting pictures began on a wet Sunday at home when I found a large square of hardboard in a cupboard under the stairs, an assortment of used artists paint tubes and one sash brush, unused.

So I dabbled with the paint. What did I know about? Ships? I painted a scene of a ship in a harbour, some sheds, dockers working cargo, old houses across the bay and the wet Sunday afternoon stretched out to two-thirty on a Monday morning.

Some days later, my picture was completed. I thought it was truly a work of art, a masterpiece – but what did others think? Was it as good as I thought or just rubbish? I asked my customers.

'Ah! Good morning, Mrs MacIntyre, twenty Embassy and the Press and Journal? That's right. By the way, Mrs MacIntyre, do you think that's a nice picture?'

So the MacIntyres, MacDonalds, Old Robbie MacIntosh and others gave comment with none suspecting I was the artist. Then Mr Frazer from one of the local hotels appeared when the shop was crowded and, while he was obliged to wait his turn, his eye fell on my picture.

'I see you're getting in some of his paintings, Bob.'

'His paintings? Whose paintings, Mr Frazer?'

‘Willie something-or-other. The Cairngorm Painter he calls himself. Aye, I always get in a few to sell to the tourists.’

Sell? Sell? He mentioned the four letter word that stimulates all shopkeepers and sets their adrenaline racing.

‘Aye, Bob,’ he went on, his nose inches from my handiwork, his eyes peering at every detail. ‘I sell them for ten pounds. But this is good. It’s worth fifteen.’

Fifteen pounds! Money! So I began painting pictures. My good friend, Denny, was the art teacher in the local school and always willing to advise and guide me over the lumpy bits of my new interest.

One day he sent round one of the top brass from the Education Authorities, an Inspector of Art or something, to pass comment on my paintings. I had seven or eight paintings arrayed on the top shelves of the shop and he studied each one briefly.

Suddenly he turned to face me. ‘You are the artist? Good. Some talent there. You are arrogant with colour. Don’t take lessons or you will lose that arrogance and your talent will go with it. Good day to you, sir.’

So my paintings sold. My hobby had become a profitable pastime and my price for a painting was seven pounds. It was also the price of a bottle of whisky in those halcyon days. My work improved when the level in my last remaining bottle was getting low.

But paintings can move people. I remember I saw a lovely black and white photograph of the Falls of Dochart at Killin, a picture where the tumbling river rolls down under the bridge. One Sunday I made a point of driving there just to see them. They say scenes can be ‘breathtakingly beautiful’ and I can find no other words to describe such beauty. I took some photographs. Back in Kingussie, I couldn’t wait to start painting the scene that was in my mind's eye. I could still see the colours, the movement and the details.

Sometimes everything goes well with a painting, everything is just right first time and that was the case in my painting of the Falls of Dochart. I finished it at one o'clock in the morning.

A few days later the wife of one of Mary's cousins saw the picture. Her back was to me while I was serving customers in the shop, then the customers left.

'Well, Ina, you like that picture? The Falls of Dochart?'

'Aye, Bob,' she answered in a small voice, pointing at the picture. 'Do you see the wee white hotel at the end of the bridge? I came all the way from Stornaway to that hotel. It was my first job, I was fourteen and I had not a single word of English in my head.'

It was then that I saw the tears in her eyes.

The inside of a country cottage was another story; an old rocking chair beside a fireplace, the mantelpiece with a clock and a window with the sunshine slanting in. I painted in a kitchen sink with some dishes at the side and a bunch of fresh flowers on the sill.

'Why don't you put someone sitting on the chair, Bob?'

This question was asked of me a few times so I returned the painting to my easel and laboured over it, trying to fit a character into that chair. My characters always seemed to end up as wooden dummies.

One day I had an emergency call to go to a ship and didn't return until ten weeks later. When I did pick up the brushes again I soon had an old man with whiskers sitting in the chair with his walking stick beside him, a pipe in his mouth and his collie lying at his feet. The picture was returned to the shelf of paintings.

It was old Mrs A.J. MacPherson who caused the fuss. She peered at it from close-up; she looked at it from six feet away then returned for another close up view.

'I know him!' She announced triumphantly to the other customers. 'I know him and one day his name will come back to me.' She bought it.

Oil paintings improve with age. They seem to become three-dimensional and colours become more alive. I saw a painting of Loch Alvie I had done, with its little white church; a painting I had sold to one of the local businessmen five years earlier and I had difficulty accepting that I had been the artist. Age had improved it so much.

There were times when I cheated a little. Like the head of a young horse whose ears never looked quite right. They looked artificial or in the wrong place. In desperation, I put a straw hat on his head and he sold quite quickly. Or the head and bare shoulders of a very beautiful lady with long hair. Her left eye was perfect, her right eye was perfect but I couldn't make her two eyes focus. She was not looking out of the picture *at* you. She was looking *through* you. So I gave this gorgeous creature an eye patch.

It sold.

One thought about painting. If you write a book you can always go into a shop and buy a copy. You can even buy a dozen copies if you so wish. But a painting is unique. You can buy photographs or a print of your painting but the painting itself is the only one there is in the whole world. When it has gone the artist seldom sees it again. I often wonder where some of my paintings are now. I wonder if their owners are kind to them.

One day, during a quiet spell, a family of four came in to look at the usual tourist novelties, postcards and newspapers. They saw my paintings. There was father in his boots, cloth cap and pipe, a very fat mother, the daughter and the boyfriend.

One painting, a stag in a forest glade with sunlight slanting through the trees, was of particular interest to the daughter.

'It's absolutely too-too gorgeous,' she gushed, 'but it just wouldn't go with our décor.'

She looked at the others on view but her eyes always returned to the one of the stag in the forest glade. Her hand floated to point at the picture and she sighed. 'So beautiful, so, so beautiful but, no, it just wouldn't go with our décor.'

Father removed his pipe from his mouth, wiped the stem under the left armpit of his jacket then pointed it at me.

'You painted that?'

'Aye, I painted it.'

'Just how long did it take you?'

'Every spare moment I had for two weeks.'

His eyes returned to the painting. 'Seven quid?'

'Aye, seven quid.'

He fumbled in his pocket for a moment, produced a wallet and counted out seven one-pound notes.

'Right, I'll take it. I like it. It'll do us just fine. The wife and I don't have any décor.'

I still have a few paintings at home but my days with hardboard and brush have long gone. I returned to writing stories.

But I still have long memories of Captain Grant Menzies. Like him, I was starting to feel the years catching up on me.

He and Lyn will have gone now. From the nightmare of being at sea in convoys when ships around you are being torpedoed and shelled and dive bombed, to tranquillity; the tranquillity of life in a Highland village. He sold newspapers and cigarettes to the adults, toys to the children and sweets to everybody. He always had pleasant words with all his customers, but I think his wife and I were the only ones he told about having to break off the head and arms and legs of a young man to get him out of a steel box built above the wing of the bridge on board his ship.

That quiet gentleman, Grant Menzies was another Merchant Navy hero I am proud to have known. Like him, I had found a way to live in peaceful retirement with my memories.

I've heard of high ranking Merchant Navy men that gave up the sea and spent their last remaining years watching television, pottering about in their garden and fighting boredom by doing the crossword in the evening paper.

They have been to sea, seen dozens of wonderful countries, met and lived on board ship with an assortment of heroes and half wits, survived blazing suns, freezing winds and can probably remember many of the terrific stories told over a few beers in a ship's smoke room.

When they retire do they ever think of writing about the wonderful, colourful life they had in the British Merchant Navy?

I woke up in darkness early one morning and tried to remember what ship I was on, but couldn't. Was the main engine a Doxford, B&W, or a Werkspoor? Or were we alongside somewhere?

It took me a few minutes to remember I was in my bed at home in 12 Highdale Road in Scarborough, eighty-three years old and hadn't put my foot on a ship in thirteen years.

THE VISIONS

1917

My mother was the seventh child of a seventh child. It is a strong belief in Scotland that the seventh child of a seventh child has 'the second sight.' Be that as it may, but I know of three occasions where it proved to be true.

She was twelve years old when she rushed to waken her mother and father in the middle of the night with screams of 'Alec has been wounded! Alec has been wounded!'

Her brother Alec was serving in France in the Great War and this was his third year in the trenches. Her mother and father calmed her, told her it was just a bad dream and Alec was not wounded at all.

Ten days later the letter arrived stating that Private Alexander Crawford, 16143, Queen's Own Cameron Highlanders, had been wounded and was now in a field hospital in France. My grandparents were amazed he was wounded on the night that their daughter, my mother, had come screaming to tell them.

Then they received a cheery letter from Alec saying that a piece of a German shell had gouged a wee bit out of his side and doctors were making a big fuss over nothing. He got lovely porridge every morning, he added.

My mother's family name was Crawford and Alec found that he was not the only Crawford among the hundreds of patients in the field hospitals in France. He found there was a Jamieson Crawford, a major in a Medical Corps of sorts in a hospital for officers less than five hundred yards away and Alec, out of sheer curiosity, went to visit him.

Jamieson was also his father's Christian name. He had never heard of anyone before, with the Christian name of 'Jamieson' and the surname of 'Crawford'. This aroused my uncle Alec's curiosity.

He hobbled his way on his crutch to find this Major Jamieson Crawford was a victim of the dreaded mustard gas. His head and hands were a mass of blisters and his eye balls were two pieces of raw flesh.

After introductions and pleasantries they soon found they had no family connections whatsoever and neither found any reason for any Crawford to have the Christian name of 'Jamieson'.

'Do your eyes hurt, sir?'

'I feel there's a roaring blow lamp pointed at each damned eye,' the Major whispered. 'I am trying hard not to scream my head off.'

A tea trolley had appeared at the end of the crowded ward.

Alec patted the Major's shoulder gently. 'Tea time, sir. Back in a moment.' He re-appeared in the crowded ward carrying two large mugs of tea without sugar or milk in either of them.

'Maybe if we wait until the tea cools a little, I could bathe your eyes, sir. It might just ease the pain.'

When the tea had cooled, he let it drip, one drop at a time, into the Major's eyes. Two more mugs of cold tea later, the Major was asleep.

This became a daily process from early morning until late evening and about fourteen days later the Major excitedly informed Alec that he could see shadows and his eyes no longer burned.

Finally the war ended, the world went back to peace and poverty and people lost contact with each other. My uncle Alec returned to being a baker in the Glasgow City

Bakeries and his father was still a precision brass moulder in Dobbies Loan in Glasgow.

1930

My grandfather's hands were crushed in an accident in the brass foundry twelve years after the war had ended. He was rushed to the Glasgow Western Infirmary where they were preparing to amputate his hands. My mother immediately had a vision, just as she had had in 1917 when Alex was wounded. I was a one-year-old baby in my mother's arms when she raced to take a tram to Alec's work place, the City Bakeries at St George's Cross. She informed Alec that their Father had had a serious accident at his work and had been rushed to the Western Infirmary. They intended to amputate his hands.

Alec raced to the Western Infirmary in the baker's van. When he arrived he found the operating theatre where preparations were under discussion. His found his father was anaesthetised and had been wheeled to the operating theatre.

They objected most strongly to a common baker's intrusion but he turned to them and roared. 'Get Jamieson Crawford here, now!'

That stopped everything. Their patient was Jamieson Crawford and the Head Surgeon in Edinburgh's Royal Infirmary was Jamieson Crawford and Alec knew this but he had never mentioned it to anyone in the past thirteen years. They telephoned Edinburgh.

So Senior Surgeon Jamieson Crawford took over the case of rebuilding my grandfather's hands. He journeyed once every week from Edinburgh to Glasgow, did most of the main operations himself and left minor side issues to the top staff at the Western Infirmary. The weeks became months, grandfather's hands were eventually in good shape, everything was very satisfactory and final tests were completed.

My uncle Alec deliberately came face to face with the Head Surgeon on his final visit to the Western Infirmary.

He spoke to him for the first time in thirteen years. 'I want to thank you, sir, for saving my father's hands.'

The Head Surgeon stepped back. 'So that is what you look like? Private Alec Crawford? You are the man who gave me my sight back in 1917. Thirteen years ago. I remember your voice. I'll always remember your voice.'

Suddenly their hands were gripped in a handshake and they stood silently looking at each other. Then the Head Surgeon finally spoke. 'Alec Crawford, for thirteen long years I have always felt I had a huge debt to pay someone I had never seen. I am pleased to think I have just paid it.'

The two men stood in the hospital corridor facing each other and the head surgeon of the Royal Infirmary in Edinburgh sighed. 'Aye, at last, sir, I have paid it in full.'

Tears sprang into his eyes and my uncle Alec watched him walk down the corridor with hospital staff in his wake.

1982

I admit that events that happened sixty or seventy years ago can alter with the passage of time.

This third vision is true and includes me.

Although I was in my fifties I still felt as fit as a bull terrier but I knew the years were catching up on me. The other engineers, apart from the Chief, were enthusiastic youngsters by comparison and we were a happy squad.

Sailing to Port Alfred, a place on the uppermost tip of the St Lawrence River in Canada then down to Georgetown in Guyana was pure hardship with river passages and fast loading and discharges. Engine maintenance and routine overhauls had fallen far behind months before we even joined and long hours were spent trying to catch up.

When I did have a sleep, I slept with my ears wide open.

Then one day, we were a long way from the mouth of the St Lawrence River when we hit a fog bank, the great grandfather of all fog banks and there were other ships moving close by.

The bridge rang 'Stand By', and then 'Slow Ahead'. This was followed by a grand assortment of movements and I could imagine the tension of those on the bridge so I stayed on the main engine controls, rather than leave them to one of the others.

If an accident happens where ships collide and there is a court case, the question arises: 'Who was on the main engine controls?'

It is better to have a fully qualified engineer officer with twenty-two years experience than a non-certificated youngster with a mere four years experience no matter how good we say he is. Consequently I took the main engine controls for twenty-six hours.

During this progress up the river, one of the units on the main engine started to 'bark' due to piston ring failure and it was debatable if there would be enough time to re-ring both pistons when we arrived.

But we did overhaul and re-ring top and bottom pistons and by that time I was hardly fit enough to make my way up from the bottom plates to the Chief's cabin. My poor bones, joints and muscles ached. I was in agony with fatigue.

There was a fat slouch of a bureaucrat in the cabin with the Chief, sitting comfortably with a beer in one hand, a lit cigarette in the other and a disdainful smirk on his face.

'Right, Chief, job's boxed up, main engine is warming through.'

The fat slouch with the disdainful smirk looked at me. He snorted. 'You look as if you might have been working.'

My eyes focussed on the Chief's wall clock. 'I have just done fifty-one hours, mister, without a break. Fifty-one hours.'

The fat slouch took a mouthful of beer then sneered. 'You, mister, probably don't know even know what hard work is.'

Suddenly sheer blind fury surged through me. I grabbed the bastard by the front of his jacket and hoisted his fifteen stone of body fat out of the chair to throw him downstairs. The Chief sprang between us and prised the slouch loose then kept his grip on me.

'STEADY, BOB, STEADY!'

The slouch flew down the stairs and sprinted off the ship like a terror-stricken spaniel. Papers headed 'The Confederated Life of Canada Insurance Company Ltd' lay scattered on the Chief's carpet.

'Are you OK, Bob?' The Chief eased his grip on me.

'Aye, Chief. I'm OK.' My heart was pounding loudly inside my chest and my clenched fists were clenched like tempered steel.

'Good. We'll let the Third take her out. You've done enough. We are sailing to New York later. Captain told me ten minutes ago.'

My mother as a child had a vision of her brother Alec being wounded in 1917. Then she had another vision in 1930 of her father's accident where his hands were crushed.

This was 1982.

When we arrived in New York, mail came on board. The letter from my mother began; 'Dear Bobby, son, I saw you! I saw you! You could have killed that fat man………'

M.V. EARL OF SKYE

As demanded by those in authority in all matters of a maritime nature, I cheerfully made my way from my home in Scarborough to Hull for a medical 'check up'. I was an able-bodied sixty-year-old, as fit as a butcher's pet bull terrier and had no qualms about the result of any medical.

But it seems I had high blood pressure. I was still fit enough for many careers in life but the Merchant Navy wasn't one of them. Evidently if a seafarer falls ill on board ship, ship owners are most reluctant to have ships alter course to the nearest port to obtain medical attention for that seafarer. It would be a financial loss for them. Again, the sick man might die if he remains on board and this would not please ship owner or seafarer either, so periodic shore side medicals are a necessity.

At sixty I felt well and fit and was most reluctant to retire and put my feet up to spend the rest of my life watching 'Coronation Street', playing darts at 'the local', or taking a dog for a walk twice a day. However, during my first forty-eight hours as a seafarer retired from all active service, my telephone rang: 'Clyde Marine Recruitment here. Ah! Mister Jackman, we believe you are now a Certificated Second Engineer Officer, retired? Would you consider 'standing by' a 20,000 ton bulk carrier at Kingston Dock? You will receive the same salary that you received as Second Engineer in Scottish Ship Management plus a generous allowance for your own self catering. It should last about three months. We also soon hope to find a Second Deck Officer and an AB to assist. Are you interested, Mister Jackman?'

'Yes! I would be very interested.'

'When can you join?'

'Kingston Dock, Glasgow, opposite the Finneston crane? I'll be on board tomorrow morning.'

'Excellent. Thank you, good-bye,' and he hung up.

Maybe retirement wouldn't be such a problem after all?

I duly arrived at Kingston Dock before noon with one suit case, one kitbag and one obliging taxi driver. We found there were two gangways, one a continuation of the other and together they made an almost vertical climb from Kingston Dock to the deck of the Earl of Skye. Window cleaners ladders are normally set up as steep as that, but gangways? Never!

This 'M.V. Earl of Skye' was a very empty 20,000 ton bulk carrier and she was as high in the water as a balloon would be in a puddle. My most obliging taxi driver earned a few extra pounds climbing that gangway with my suit case while I followed with my kit bag and we both stood for quite a while, wheezing on the main deck, fighting to get our breaths back.

He left, wished me luck, and I made my way to the Chief Engineer's accommodation. It boasted a large dayroom, a bathroom with shower and a good sized bedroom. All the cupboards and drawers were empty except those in the desk and they held nothing of any consequence.

I sat down to recover a little more then put on a boiler suit and checked over the diesel generator purring away merrily on the main deck. It was being fed from a fuel tank I judged to be about seven tons capacity and proving to be about 90% full. Engine room bilges were empty, nothing was missing and there were no strangers lurking in dark corners. I was alone.

With promises of full pay plus catering payments for doing very little, I was beginning to enjoy this retirement business.

There was an outside telephone on board in the top alleyway and I could hear from my cabin if it rang.

I heard it ring at nine o'clock on my first morning on board. 'Hello? Mr Jackman? Clyde Marine Recruitment here. There is a Second Mate on his way to the ship. He should be with you in less than an hour. He has a companion with him. Is everything to your satisfaction, Mr Jackman?'

'Yes, everything is okay.'

'Good-bye.'

So I waited out on deck until a taxi appeared at the far end of the dock then carefully made my way down the vertical gangways to give the newcomers a welcome and assist with their luggage.

That's when I met Gary and his companion. He was in his mid-twenties and smiled easily. His companion was a long legged blonde who chewed gum thoughtfully and didn't smile. Her eyes slid over me briefly then she made her way to the gangway without even offering to carry anything. She moved slowly upwards, carefully holding the gangway hand rails.

I struggled close behind her with a suitcase, Gary followed me with other luggage and where this climb up the gangway had me breathless carrying my own luggage previously, I was twice as breathless on this occasion. This time I broke into a sweat as well.

It was 1990, when mini skirts were in fashion and I was climbing the gangway fourteen inches behind her. She was wearing the tiniest mini skirt that hid nothing and it didn't do my blood pressure any good at all. I flopped down on deck and waited for Gary.

However we settled in with my two new crew members moving into the First Mate's cabin, despite his companion's insistence that she wanted the Captain's suite.

We intended taking turns at cooking and shopping but she wouldn't cook, Gary couldn't cook but they bought tinned food or fish and chips so they didn't starve. She seemed to exist on chocolate biscuits and Coca-Cola and I did my own shopping and cooking.

Neither of them seemed to know how to wash dishes either though Gary did try a few times in their early days.

There was a laundry room in the officers' accommodation complete with a washing machine, tumble drier, ironing board and other washing equipment.

In her second week, Gary's mini-skirted companion forced so much clothing and bed linen into the washing machine that the door wouldn't shut. She forced it and when she had it almost shut she started the machine. Consequently it battered itself to death and the laundry room was awash by the time she found Gary.

I was working in the bottom of the engine room when Gary found me and the water was by then streaming all through the accommodation.

It was shortly after that that Gary decided his erotic, nocturnal pleasures with his companion no longer took precedence over the blunders and cock-ups made by her in the daylight hours. He sent her back home to Edinburgh, but visited her on Saturday nights and returned on Sunday mornings. But Sunday mornings soon lengthened to became Sunday evenings. Then one Sunday evening became a very late Monday morning and a top manager of Clyde Marine arrived with our pay cheques. I was boiler suited and coming out of the engine room when we came face-to-face.

His voice was decidedly cold. ‘I’ve been searching the ship for that Second Mate. Is he on board?’

‘Gary? It’s lunchtime. He probably nipped up to Govan Road to buy us a couple of pizzas.’

Who believes in miracles in the twentieth century? No shortage of them in biblical times and maybe a few in the last hundred years but this was my first ever experience of one.

The door at the end of the alleyway opened and Gary clambered in, carrying two pizzas. The first time, the only time, ever he brought pizzas on board.

A week later Gary was given a golden opportunity to join a French Cruise liner and he left.

His relief proved to be a Big Slouch with a slack mouth whose name I am pleased to have forgotten. The first thing he did was move the telephone and its table from the top deck to sit at his cabin door. Then he sat in his cabin and read paper back books with his door wide open.

Two days later I found he had Gary’s companion living with him. It was early morning when the Big Slouch happened to come out of his cabin, meet me in the alleyway and forget he had left his cabin door wide open. She was sitting up in the bunk with a paperback book in her hand and was so engrossed in it she didn’t realise I was looking straight at her from where I was standing.

She didn’t see me so it must have been a helluva exciting book.

Big Slouch didn’t last very long. A few days went by, Clyde Marine did some research into his past, found he was ‘not suitable’ and requested he found employment elsewhere. He left.

Gary’s ex-companion slipped into my cabin and closed the door quietly. I slipped her out of my cabin and I, too, closed the door quietly.

A few days passed before Clyde Marine phoned again. 'We have another Second Mate, Mr Jackman, a young man called 'Sladovitch' and he has all the correct qualifications. Good references too.'

I had sailed with a Captain Sladovitch in the past and I remember he had his wife and two boys with him on one trip. That was nearly twenty years ago. The Captain was a very competent ship's officer, his wife was a perfect lady and I taught their sons how to do card tricks and how to play pontoons.

When the office manager brought this new Second Mate to me to introduce us, I looked at them both and shook my head. 'Do I have to sail with ***him*** again?'

There was a long, slow intake of breath from the agent and he looked at each of us singly. 'You know Mr Sladovich? You have been with him before?'

I laughed to stem his worries. 'His father, Captain Slad, was one of the finest captains I ever sailed with. He took his wife and two sons along on a trip to America and Canada and I was Second Engineer then.'

'You're Black Bob!' He gripped me by the shoulders and nearly jumped up and down in excitement.

'Aye, and if you turn out to be half as good a Captain as your father, you'll be a damn good Captain indeed.'

He was three weeks with me on the 'Earl of Skye' before leaving to join Shell tankers and I was sorry to see him go.

I had earned the title of 'Black Bob' during eighteen month stretches on the China Coast nightmare coal run where winches were used and abused by commando dockers working on shifts, twenty-four hours per day. Meanwhile, maintaining the ship's engines plus overhauling the shattered winches in freezing winter conditions caused me being often covered in coal dust and earned me my title.

Another title, or nick name, I inherited was 'Popeye'. When I sailed with Guyanese crew, it was the practice in that old ship to take a 14lb hammer and spanner and tighten all cylinder head nuts on the main engine at 'Full Away.' The Guyanese were very muscular and a lot taller than me but I never had any problems swinging a 14lb hammer.

I had always been a heavy smoker but cigarettes in an antiquated engine room were a problem so I turned to using a light weight Falcon aluminium stemmed pipe and kept it clenched between my teeth when working. When I belted that spanner, a lovely smoke ring came up from the bowl of that pipe at every wallop.

So they called me 'Popeye' and I had that name for years.

To continue with nick names, the mynah bird is the blackest and dirtiest bird in the bird world and it is also the greatest talker. It seldom shuts up. In Hindustani, the Indian crew often refer to the Second Engineer Officer as the '**manshla mynah sahib.'**

I have corrected many. Second Engineer Officer is the '**manshla mistri sahib.'** When they spoke about me, they always emphasized the word **'mistri'** meaning 'engineer,' and I think they appreciated the fact I bothered to learn a bit of their language.

Months passed pleasurably, people came and went, and four high rank engineers came from Upper Clyde Shipbuilders to pass judgement on the engine room. They informed me that the MV Earl of Skye would be converted to being a sheep carrier, re-designed to carry sheep from New Zealand or Australia to the Persian Gulf.

Suddenly there was a whole ship's crew on board, officers and ratings galore and I found myself now transferred from the elegant Chief's cabin to a small cabin near the bridge often used for pilots. The gangway was improved and no longer a test for Alpine climbers. Luggage blocked alleyways and everyone talked at once.

My days on the 'Earl of Skye' were over. They were many days and they were happy days. I had enjoyed fifteen very pleasant months on board, the first fifteen months of my retirement from the Merchant Navy and many others were to follow.

Summing up, for those that retired after a life of sailing all over the world, don't just talk about your seafaring days and the wonderful characters you sailed with, write about them!

If you can write about the heroes and half wits you sailed with over the years, you are writing great stories.

'Merchant Navy Heroes and Half Wits' earned six reviews in its first month on the open market. (Five reviews were from Merchant Navy Heroes, one review was from a Half Wit.)

Our Mate, or Chief Officer as he insisted being entitled, didn't like the Scots very much and being rude to those who were Scots gave him great pleasure.

I, on the other hand, was a twenty-seven year old Second Engineer Officer, born and reared in Glasgow and wise enough not to take offence since it would only cause bad feeling among the others on board our happy ship. Bad feelings in any ship's crowded smoke room are never welcome. They could lead to problems and bloody noses.

'Well, you know what they say about the Scots,' our fat twit of a Mate smirked, looking round the faces of the others for confirmation but finding none.

'We know what the English say about the Scots.' Chief Engineer Officer, Jim Weir, paused as he lit his pipe to pass the remark and then continued: 'You see, Matey, you English have a poor idea of what education is all about and you nonchalantly omit facts or alter those that are non-flattering. To put it bluntly, the English hide the truth if it doesn't please them.'

The Mate's face went pink and there were a few giggles. 'I had two years in a university so you can't say I am not educated.'

He looked round the others but only a few deck juniors nodded in agreement. The others in the crowded smokeroom avoided his look.

The Chief studied the bowl of his pipe for a moment then smiled at the Mate. 'You consider yourself to be educated, Matey? Well, one of the most important names that the English like to avoid is 'Nellie Wallace.' Tell me what you know about 'Nellie Wallace' and we shall see what you learned, or didn't learn, in your English university.'

'Nellie Wallace? Nellie Wallace?' The Mate spluttered. 'Who in the hell was Nellie Wallace?'

The Chief pointed the stem of his pipe at the Mate's nose. 'The story of the 'Nellie Wallace' should have rammed up the left nostril of every English politician that ever parked his backside in the House of Commons, but as I said earlier, the English prefer to omit certain facts in their history lessons.'

The Chief finished his beer and I had two beers ready for us to avoid any delay in his onslaught. 'Carry on, Chief, you are doing well even if we are outnumbered.'

'Aye, Bob, it just so happens that my mother was Scots. Anyway, to continue with hopeless task of educating our Mate, the Clyde was getting a great reputation for building ships with engines in them. Henry Bell built the first successful one when he built the 'Comet' in 1812 and there were others. 'Lucy Ashton', 'Jeannie Deans' and oh! I can't remember the names of others, but I do remember the 'Nea Hellas'. Nea Hellas is Greek for 'New Greece, but the Clydesiders called her the 'Nellie Wallace'. She was still a sailing ship, but one with an engine as well. An experimental steam engine.'

The Mate interrupted the Chief. 'She had sails as well as an engine? I don't believe it.'

'You would believe it if you had been educated, Matey.'

The Mate scowled and turned his head away but still kept one eye on the Chief.

After a moment spent lighting his pipe, the Chief continued. 'It was the time of another potato famine in Ireland where thousands of poor Irish peasants were dying of starvation every day. England was the richest country in

Great Britain and they left the peasants in the Irish part of Great Britain to starve to death. Men, women and children died of hunger.'

There wasn't a sound in the smoke room. At that moment one of the Indian stewards came into the smoke room through the pantry door and he was silently ushered back out again.

'It was the practice in those days that any ship built on the Clyde did a trip round Ireland and back to the Clyde to prove its seaworthiness. When the 'Nellie Wallace' was nearing completion one of the workers came up with the idea of putting food on board for the Irish people. It was agreed they could stop her briefly in Cork and discharge it all. It was a great idea and all the workers in the shipyards had their wives buy groceries and they stowed them on board. Then, when the Clydeside shopkeepers learned this, they gave them whole boxes of food, and then the wholesalers joined in with more food. The 'Nellie Wallace' ended up with tons of food on board for the starving people in Ireland. That food was given by the ordinary working class people that lived on the Clydeside, Mate, Clydeside working class Scots.'

The Chief stopped long enough to wet his whistle with beer number three and then went on. 'Just before she was due for her test run round Ireland, a bus arrived with some soldiers, deck officers and an English Captain. Only the ship's engineers that had built the engine and some ordinary seamen remained on board. Steam was raised, the engines were warmed through, the 'Nellie Wallace' left the berth and sailed to Ireland. But she didn't stop at Cork to discharge the food. They took her all the way round Ireland, stopped at Greenock on the Clyde and threw all the food over the side. They threw all the food the Scots had put on board then sailed all the way up to Yorkhill Quay in

Glasgow. The stand-by crew with their Captain left the ship in dead silence, escorted by the soldiers. They boarded the buses waiting for them at the dock gates and not one of them even looked back.'

Jim Weir moved over and put his empty beer glass on the bar, turned to face-to-face with the Mate and smiled. 'Now you know what others say about the Scots, Matey, and what other people say about the English. Good night!'

He left the bar and made his way up to his cabin.

I stayed a little longer to see how the others re-acted to the Chief's tale about the 'Nellie Wallace' and all the lads, Scots, English and others were discussing it quietly.

The Mate yawned loudly, stretched, said 'Goodnight everybody', but he was ignored by all.

I downed my beer, said 'Goodnight, everybody' and had cheery replies from the others.

The Chief's cabin door was open when I came into the alleyway.

He called, 'Bob, let's have a nightcap.' He had two glasses at the ready and an open bottle of Bells poised over them.

I sat down, he poured. 'Well, what did you think of my story?'

'Your story?'

'Yes, my story. It was just a story, pure fiction, all lies. I was making it up as I went along. The Irish Famine was from 1845 to 1852. The Nea Hellas wasn't built until 1922 and was built in Fairfield's Shipyard. She was a luxury liner that could carry 2500 passengers. There was not a Nea Hellas of any kind at the time of the Irish Famine. As I say, it was all one big fairy tale I made up for two reasons. First, I wanted to shut the Mate up. Different nationalities among the lads don't matter on board ships, they only cause trouble. On board ship you are all one family, you are shipmates whether you like it or not and awkward characters like the Mate deserve to get their backsides kicked, metaphorically speaking. I repeat, all one family.'

He stopped talking to charge the glasses. 'I have another reason, Bob, and I'll tell you what it is. I am retiring at the end of this year and I want to take up writing books about the Merchant Navy. I'll find a Writers Club of some kind. I just want something to do at home when I'm retired. I've had forty-five years at sea and I'll *need* something to do, other than watch telly, or listen to what the wife says about the neighbours or play darts at the 'local, or.....' He paused. 'How old are you, Bob?'

'Me? I am twenty-seven. But I could never write a book, Chief. No, I could never write a book.'

It seems I was wrong, doesn't it? This is my fourth.

MY FINALE

This ends my fourth and final book about my life in the Merchant Navy. I am proud to say I have joined the ranks of other Merchant Navy writers, writers like John Lee, David Hucknall, Norman Freeman, Bernard Edwards, David Baboulene and others too numerous to mention.

But what a world we have written about. Names of the lads I sailed with still spring to mind, even back to my first ship in Nourse Line, the MV Marjata, in July 1950, up to my departure from seafaring in the luxurious passenger cruiser, the 'Hebridean Princess' in 1990.

Our years in the Merchant Navy gave us a vast supply of events to write about, the kaleidoscope of colourful characters we sailed with, the happenings on board the ship at sea, the wilds of African ports, the mysteries of the West Indies, the sheer luxuries of Japan and China etc. The list is endless.

Compare that world with those who sit at an office desk shuffling papers for eight hours per day, through the years until they finally retire. Could they find something in their working lives worth writing about? Could those poor souls write a story of an all-night session in Hong Kong, or a typhoon in the Pacific, or the time the cook fell overboard? (He didn't fall, he was pushed.)

Perhaps not, but they would willingly read about it.

There are so many ex-bureaucratic, geriatric pensioners spending their remaining years with the evening newspaper and the excitement of watching programmes on the telly. That's their life, a life of doing nothing very slowly, but it's not the life of those that sailed the seven seas and saw the world, so write about it.

'Me? Oh, I could never write a book!'

I've been told that so often by so many.

To begin:-

1) Write a title.
2) Write the first sentence.
3) Write the first paragraph.
4) Write the first page.
5) Write your first book.
6) Then write it again.

No one does it differently. You go back over it, changing words here and there, alter the plot a little, bring in a new character and throw in a bit of love life with a fair young maid, whoopee!

If you think that is a load of rubbish, William Shakespeare did it and it gave him his terrific success in the theatre world. He would sharpen a goose quill feather to a point, dip it into his home made ink and write it all down on parchment that was as rough as an old army blanket. Each player on the stage would need to be given a handwritten copy.

When a theatre two miles away wanted the same play he would write it again and polish it up even more. Each time he wrote that play, he improved it and by the time he had re-written it six times for six different theatres, it was a terrific play and certainly far superior to the one that he wrote the first time.

And if he can do it, so can you.

I think William Shakespeare did eventually become quite famous. If he did, why don't you? I repeat, <u>why don't you?</u>

THE THEFT OF ORDONNANCE

(I won a London Poetry Competition with this.)

Thoughts just out of reach.
Dreams in the busy daylight hours.
Glimpses of those but faintly remembered.
On the distant fringes of this, I live my tangible life.

Should I awake and join this tangible world?
Or am I awake? Which world is mine?
I hear music. Mere wisps of melodies long forgotten.
Their sweetness fills me still and I lie content.

Age is lowering its dark velvet mantle over me.
Beneath its dark folds I smile,
And patiently await the silence.

THE END

5036653R00056

Printed in Great Britain
by Amazon.co.uk, Ltd.,
Marston Gate.